A Passion for Preaching

A Passion for Preaching

Reflections on the Art
of Preaching
Essays in Honor of
Stephen F. Olford
Compiled by David L. Olford

Thomas Nelson Publishers
Nashville

Published in Nashville, Tennessee, by Thomas Nelson, Inc., and distributed in Canada by Lawson Falle, Ltd., Cambridge, Ontario.

Printed in the United States of America.

Library of Congress Cataloging-in-Publication Data

A Passion for preaching : essays in honor of Stephen F. Olford /
   compiled by David L. Olford.
       p.   cm.
   Includes bibliographical references.
   ISBN 0-8407-7246-7
   1. Preaching 2. Olford, Stephen F. I. Olford, Stephen F.
II. Olford, David L. (David Lindsay)
BV4211.2.P27   1989
251—dc20   89-27037
                          CIP

1 2 3 4 5 6 — 93 92 91 90 89

Contents

Foreword

This book honors my father, Stephen F. Olford, a man with a passion for preaching. The idea for this book came to mind a number of years ago. My academic studies included the reading of a number of books of collected articles. Often these books honored noted scholars on special occasions in their lives, and the contents of the books usually reflected the interests of the honored person.

This book, in a preliminary form, was presented to my father on a very special occasion. The contributors to the book are colleagues in the ministry, my brother, and myself. Originally the contributors were given the broad subject areas of preaching, evangelism, or revival, all of these being concerns of my father's. Tributes, articles, and sermons have been offered on a variety of topics within the broader subject areas. The structure chosen for the contents came much later in the light of what was contributed. (The message by my father was added later also.) This book, therefore, is not a comprehensive treatment of a subject. It is an expression of love and respect to a man who cares deeply about the topics and issues addressed by this book. The book honors a preacher and the type of ministry and message he represents.

The first time my father knew anything about this book was when I presented a bound copy of the contributed manuscripts to him at a special dinner in Memphis, Tennessee, on June 3, 1988. This wonderful evening was a time of celebration of God's faithfulness over seventy years of my father's life, forty years of marriage, and almost fifty years of ministry. The celebration on June 3 was followed the next day by a service of dedication for the Stephen Olford Center for Biblical Preaching, established in Memphis.

My father asked Billy Graham to send a word of greeting to be read at the service of dedication, since he could not be present. Dr. Graham's appropriate and challenging words appear at the end of this foreword. His 7

prayer for that special occasion was that it would be a time of commitment, "a day of dedication" for all who were present. It is my prayer that
the reading of this book will be a time of commitment and dedication for
each reader. I pray that this book challenges, inspires, and directs readers
to be committed to the type of ministry and message that my father has
carried out through the years. Most importantly, I hope and pray that this
book will encourage a greater personal commitment to our Lord and Savior, Jesus Christ.

I am thankful for all those who have encouraged this project or directly
participated in it. I want to thank, first of all, each contributor. Whether
the material was written previously or for this book specifically, the offering was an act of love and sacrifice.

Due to other commitments, a number of people who were asked could
not contribute to this volume, so I am especially thankful that so many
were able to respond. You will find their names listed on the page of
contributors. One of our contributors, Dr. Alan Redpath, passed on to be
with the Lord on March 17, 1989. We thank God upon every remem-
brance of his life and ministry.

I need to thank many other people who have been involved in this tribute project. Janet Olson and Mark Boorman helped with proofreading and
editing at an early stage in the project—thank you! Ellen Dickson typed
hundreds of pages of manuscripts, and she handled much correspondence
relevant to this volume—thank you! Victoria Kuhl has carefully gone
through each manuscript and helped with editing. She also gave many
helpful suggestions concerning the book and compiled the biographical
profile concerning my father's life, writings, and distinctions—thank you!
Volunteers and members of the Encounter Ministries, Inc., staff have in
various ways helped in this project. This has been a group effort and I am
grateful—thank you all!

A special paragraph of thanks is due to Thomas Nelson Publishers.
First, my thanks to Bruce Barbour for agreeing to take on this project.
My thanks to Randy Elliot for all his ideas and input as well as time taken
to facilitate the project. My thanks, also, to Jennifer Farrar for her edito-
rial work along with others assigned to review these manuscripts. My
thanks to all involved in bringing about the final product.

This book is a tribute and "thank you" to my father, and I will let the
contents do that, including the tributes by my brother and myself. Any
book that honors my father in a real sense must honor my mother as well.

The majority of my father's life and ministry have been shared at the deepest level with my mother, "together with God." So, although this book is not a tribute to my mother directly, I pay her tribute here, and recognize her vital role in my father's life. My mother knew about this project long before my father did, and she has been behind it completely. I want to thank her for her support, and for the idea of including in the book something written by my father. (My father's message gives expression at least in part to his understanding of and passion for preaching.)

I want to say thank you also to my brother for so personally and appropriately paying tribute to our father. Then, as I conclude, I want to thank my beloved friend and wife, Ellen. Ellen has been very supportive of this book from the start, and she has been a constant source of encouragement to me along the way.

Now and forever, thanks be to God and "to Him be glory" (Eph. 3:21).

David Lindsay Olford
Memphis, Tennessee
July 1989

I regret that I will be overseas in June and thus cannot join you as you dedicate the Stephen Olford Center for Biblical Preaching.

We give thanksgiving to God that He has led in the vision for this Center, and in the plans and preparations that bring you to this special day.

It is my prayer that it will not only be a day of dedication of a building and programs—but especially of people. There are some of you present today who are staff and support workers at the Center who will want to commit yourselves firstly to the Lord, and then to the ministry that lies before you; others are interested friends whose commitment will be a promise of faithful prayer support and interest; others may even be here out of curiosity and may never have committed your lives to Jesus Christ as Lord and Savior. For you this may be a day of dedication of yourselves in a new way.

May God bless each of you, and especially our beloved friends Stephen and Heather Olford, for whom the Center is named. We continue to thank God for his hand upon their lives—for the tremendous way he has blessed and used them down through the years in Britain and here in the United States. It is my prayer that he will honor their vision here today, and bless the use to which the Center is dedicated.

Cordially yours,

Billy

Billy Graham

Dedicatory Prayer

Our Lord and our God, we honor Thee.

We give Thee, dearest Lord, glory, . . .
                                    majesty, . . .
                                    reverence.

We bless Thee.
   We extol Thee.
      We lift Thee, our Lord God, in praise on this beautiful day.

We adore Thee—
   Father, . . .
      Son, . . .
         and Holy Ghost.

Lord, for the beauty of this day, and for the beauty of this place,
   for the warmth of our fellowship,
      for the presence of our dear Savior,
we bless Thy holy Name.

And now, our Lord, we come to dedicate
   a place . . . and a purpose.
Our Father, we dedicate this ministry to Thyself. Lord, it is Thine, and
of Thine own have we given unto Thee, for, Lord, we know that
   from Thee . . .
      and through Thee, . . .
         and to Thee
are all things. And then, our Father God, we do dedicate this ministry
not only to Thyself, but, Lord, to the purpose to which it has been set
aside. By the eye of faith, Lord, we see changed lives, . . .
                                    changed churches, . . .
                                    saved souls;
Lord, a ministry of Your Word around the world where preachers,
   with a head full of scriptural knowledge,
      and a heart on fire,
         and a tongue—the tongue of the learned—
are willing to declare Your Word. God, grant that that shall be so.

And our Father God, we therefore dedicate ourselves to Thyself,
　to prayer, . . .
　　to holy living.
　Lord, one more time—anew and afresh—as much as in us is, Lord, we give ourselves unto Thee, our Lord. Holy Spirit of God, as You inhabit our humanity, display Your deity, and may the living of our lives be the living of Your life in us—
　　　　　　　　　and through us;
and Lord, together—now—with joy and solemnity,
　　　　　　　　　with faith and anticipation,
these grounds . . .
　this ministry . . .
is Thine, O God, for Thy glory, and in the name of Jesus,

Amen!

Dr. Adrian Rogers
Pastor, Bellevue Baptist Church
Memphis, Tennessee
June 4, 1988
Dedication of Stephen Olford Center
　for Biblical Preaching

CONTRIBUTORS

Rev. W. Ian Barclay is an Anglican clergyman who serves on the staff of The Evangelical Alliance (U.K.) as Secretary to the Churches Department. He is president of British Youth for Christ and vice president of the Nurses' Christian Fellowship.

Dr. D. Stuart Briscoe is a popular author, conference speaker, and since 1970, pastor of Elmbrook Church, Brookfield, Wisconsin.

Dr. W. A. Criswell has pastored the First Baptist Church of Dallas, Texas, since 1944, and has been president of the Southern Baptist Convention. He is editor of the *Criswell Study Bible*.

Dr. Joel C. Gregory is senior pastor of the Travis Avenue Baptist Church, Fort Worth, Texas, and former assistant professor of homiletics at Southwestern Baptist Theological Seminary. He is an author, lecturer, and convention speaker.

Dr. Gerald B. Griffiths is former pastor of Calvary Church, Toronto, Canada, and serves as chairman of the International Council of the Africa Inland Mission. He is a widely traveled conference speaker, lecturer, and author.

Rev. Philip Hacking is vicar of Christ Church, Fulwood, Sheffield, England. He also serves as chairman of the English Keswick Convention.

Dr. James M. Latimer is senior minister of Central Church, Memphis, Tennessee, and chancellor of Crichton College, located on the campus of Central Church.

Dr. David Olford is vice president of Encounter Ministries, Inc., director of studies for the Institute for Biblical Preaching at the Stephen Olford Center, Memphis, Tennessee, and editor of *The Preacher,* the quarterly publication of Encounter.

Mr. Jonathan Olford served for several years as a missionary in Kenya, East Africa. He is currently pursuing doctoral studies in clinical psychology in Chicago to prepare for future ministry.

Dr. Stephen F. Olford (see Profile, p. 21)

Dr. William L. Probasco is pastor of MeadowBrook Baptist Church, Gadsden, Alabama, and minister-at-large of Christian Ministry Resources.

Dr. Alan Redpath pastored two churches in the British Isles and was the former minister of Moody Memorial Church, Chicago. During his lifetime, he also was an evangelist, conference speaker, and author. Dr. Redpath died in March, 1989.

Dr. Paul S. Rees, a former pastor, has served as vice president-at-large for World Vision, Inc., and was director for many of their Pastors' Conferences. He has spoken in more than sixty countries, and has written numerous books and articles.

Dr. Ted S. Rendall has served in various capacities on the staff of Prairie Bible Institute, Three Hills, Alberta, Canada, which named him its president in March, 1986. He is also senior pastor of the Prairie Tabernacle Congregation and the author of several books.

Dr. Haddon W. Robinson is president of Denver Conservative Baptist Seminary, a nationally known speaker throughout the United States and Canada, and a gifted writer. His book on biblical preaching is now used as a text for preaching in ninety seminaries and Bible colleges in North America.

Dr. Paul B. Smith is senior minister of The People's Church, Toronto, Canada, an evangelist, Bible teacher, noted missionary leader, and author.

Dr. Charles F. Stanley is pastor of the First Baptist Church of Atlanta, Georgia, and a former president of the Southern Baptist Convention. His nationwide radio and television program, *In Touch,* is heard and seen by millions each week. He has written several books and serves on the Board of Directors of the National Religious Broadcasters Association.

Dr. Ray C. Stedman has been the pastor of Peninsula Bible Church, Palo Alto, California, since 1950 where he emphasizes a strong training program for laymen and ministers. A prolific writer, he serves on the board of numerous Christian organizations.

Major W. Ian Thomas is founder and general director of the Capernwray Missionary Fellowship of Torchbearers in northwest England, and Conference Centers and Bible Schools in many parts of the world. He has been involved in an evangelistic and Bible teaching ministry.

Part 1:
Preaching: God's Man

Profile of Stephen F. Olford
1918—

S tephen F. Olford was born on March 29, 1918, to Britisher Frederick Ernest Samuel Olford and American Elizabeth "Bessie" Rho-
den Santmire Olford.

As the son of missionaries, Stephen Olford spent the first seventeen years of his life on a mission station in West Africa, witnessing first-
hand the power of the gospel to change lives. He received his early
education under the private tutelage of a graduate of Bristol University for
his Oxford Extension Matriculation Exams. Upon returning to England
he studied engineering at Devonport Technical College, but a motorcycle
accident precipitated a spiritual crisis, leading him to take up theological
training at St. Luke's College in Mildmay, London, and later at the Missionary Training Colony in Upper Norwood, a suburb of London. He also
took courses through the London School of Journalism and the Moody
Bible Institute Correspondence School in Chicago.

Following college days he engaged in evangelistic work in the villages
of England until the outbreak of war in 1939.

During World War II he served as an Army Scripture Reader with the
troops at a servicemen's center in Newport, South Wales. He was also a
leader of the Young People's Christian Fellowship, an inter-
denominational work in Newport which rapidly became a center of spiritual witness, evangelistic outreach, and missionary interest throughout
the Welsh principality.

At the end of the war he resumed crusading in many of the major cities
of the British Isles, Canada, and the United States, and was a frequent
speaker at English Keswick, Hildenborough Hall, and similar centers on
both sides of the Atlantic.

In 1948 he married Barbara Heather Brown, whom he met when he
came to her native Ireland for evangelistic meetings. Over the years her
prayer ministry, wise counsel, and gracious dignity have made her the

ideal pastor's wife. They have two sons—Jonathan and David. Jonathan and his wife, Catherine, live in Illinois and are parents to Jeremy David and Justin Stephen. Jonathan, after several years of missionary service in Kenya, East Africa, is pursuing doctoral studies; David, who is Vice President of Encounter Ministries, Inc., lives with his wife, Ellen, in Memphis.

Ordained in October 1953, Stephen Olford served for six years as pastor of Duke Street Baptist Church, Richmond, Surrey, England (1953–1959), followed by fourteen years as senior minister of Calvary Baptist Church, New York City (1959–1973). During this period the radio outreach was expanded worldwide. A television ministry was launched in October 1960 which continued for the next fifteen years. Dr. Olford established Keswick conventions in strategic locations throughout the United States, Canada, and the Caribbean; initiated the New York School of the Bible to train laymen in theology, evangelism, and soul-winning; found time to conduct citywide crusades; and authored numerous books, booklets, and articles.

In recognition of the way he articulated the biblical message, Dr. Olford was awarded the following doctorates: Doctor of Divinity, Wheaton College (1966) and Dallas Baptist University (1983); Doctor of Letters, Houghton College (1966); and Doctor of Humanities, Richmond College (1975). He earned a Doctor of Theology degree from Luther Rice Seminary in 1978 and lectures there annually.

In 1970, while continuing to maintain the busy program of the church, Dr. Olford formally launched Encounter Ministries to fulfill the Great Commission through media, ministry, and missionary outreach. Following his resignation from Calvary Baptist Church, he set up Encounter headquarters in Holmes Beach, Florida, later moving his ministry to Wheaton, Illinois, and, most recently, to Memphis, Tennessee.

In 1980 he opened the Institute for Biblical Preaching to help restore expository preaching to the pulpit. He also conducts preaching institutes on both sides of the Atlantic to encourage and equip pastors and laymen in the work of the ministry.

Dr. Billy Graham considers Stephen Olford as "the greatest combination of pastor, teacher, and evangelist he has ever known in the Christian ministry," and "the man who has most influenced [his] ministry." Dr. Olford has shared the platform with Dr. Graham in numerous conferences and congresses: Montreux, Switzerland (1960); Berlin, Germany

(1966); Lausanne, Switzerland (1974); and Amsterdam, Holland (1983, 1986). Others feel Dr. Olford is "the prince of expositors for our time." He stands tall in the pulpit as an ambassador for Christ, his supreme passion being to "preach the gospel to every creature." Like his namesake in the Acts of the Apostles, he is a man "full of faith, full of the Holy Spirit, full of wisdom, full of grace, and full of power."

A Tribute to Stephen F. Olford— as a Father

JONATHAN M. OLFORD

"Children's children are the crown of old men,
And the glory of children is their father."
Proverbs 17:6

The responsibility of preparing this tribute to Stephen F. Olford has represented both a challenge and a privilege. Like his many admirers throughout the United States and overseas, my remembrances of my father are many and varied, both shared and intimate. The challenge has been how to communicate, in a few short words, a sense of that which has been most meaningful. The privilege, perhaps more obvious, is that I have the opportunity to present this tribute to the man who has meant more to me in my lifetime than any other.

As I pondered the event of a seventieth birthday and the inevitable soul-searching that must come with it, I began to wonder. As I am sure my father has done, I have reviewed the multitude of years he has spent in the pastoral ministry and all of his additional years of effective extended ministry through the work of Encounter. In addition to his pulpit and conference preaching, he has touched many lives through radio outreach, and I have experienced personally the warmth and fellowship we have shared through the power of that radio ministry while nestled some ten thousand miles from home in the highlands of Kenya. His writing has touched still others. Through the devotional insights of little booklets such as *Manna in the Morning* to the fuller expositions exemplified by *Camping With God* and *I'll Take the High Road,* he has touched hearts and lives through the power of the Holy Spirit enabling people to experience the saving power of the Lord Jesus Christ and the deeper victorious Christian life available to those who know and trust Him. However, I want to look be-

24

yond the great ministry of Stephen Olford in order to share what has been of utmost importance to me. This weekend of celebration and dedication is a landmark experience for my father, representing many years of personal sojourn and pilgrimage on this earth, manifold years of ministry, and numerous years of faithful companionship in loving relationship with my mother. What is most meaningful to me is the personal relationship I have had with my dad, for had that not been something to remember—had the reality of his preaching, commitment, and life story not been represented in his personal relationship with me—I'm afraid all the rest would have been waste. He has been called the "Prince of Preachers," "one of the most powerful preachers of the twentieth century," and "the preacher's Preacher." Over the course of fifty years of ministry many changes have taken place. The focus of the ministry has altered. The geographical location of the organization has varied. The very purpose of the ministry has even changed subtly. However, through all of the transformations and evolutions that have taken place in the life and ministry of Dr. Stephen F. Olford, the title that has stood the test of time—and the one I prefer the most—is "Dad."

As the father of two sons myself, I now look back at the years of my youth in search of a role model. By the grace of God I don't have to look very far. Having worked with young people and having studied psychology intensively, I have a heightened awareness of the validity of this need and the increased responsibility for parents to fulfill this requirement within the Christian community. In an age of compromise, smoke screen commitments, and cheap sentiment, my father provided my brother and me with love, nurture, care, and a commodity deemed rare today: attention and time. As I daily commit my own responsibilities of fatherhood to the Lord in prayer, requesting wisdom, patience, and the ability to provide my children with my best, I often find myself drawn back in time to my childhood and adolescence in New York. Perhaps a narrative or an anecdotal study might express the thought more effectively.

Saturday was always the busiest day of the week. I know any pastor can identify with this regardless of the number of sermons that he is to preach on Sunday, or of the number of services he must oversee. As I recall our years in "the city," I remember Saturday as the day with Dad. Waking up on Saturday morning usually meant breakfast cooked by Dad, with such delights on the menu as any "leftovers" in the refrigerator that could be mixed with rice, an egg or two, and fried in the frying pan. This cuisine stemmed from his own African experience, and I must say it was something we never tired of. In addition, it is a treat my four-year-old and I continue to share. Usually, breakfast was followed by a trip to the park, a walk down Fifth Avenue, or a couple of hours in the New York Athletic Club, a privilege authorized by the kindness of a lifetime member who had been touched by my father's ministry. In this case, we all benefited by spending occasional Saturday mornings in the cold of winter happily shooting baskets, swimming, or playing hand tennis and badminton.

As the day progressed, preparations for the Lord's Day became of the utmost importance, and my father would seclude himself in his study for preparation. Yet, even with the pressures of the following day, I don't remember a time when my dad became unapproachable or unavailable; he took fatherhood seriously. My brother and I were blessings to my parents, not inconveniences to be worked around in the interest of business, career, or church accomplishments, however spiritual they might have seemed. The very fact that this was communicated so clearly is significant to me now. Thus, even when things were the busiest, Dad had time for us. Certainly there were times when his study door was closed, but it was never locked, and while he was not always able to immediately spend the time to completely work through our concerns, he was willing and able to give us of himself. His availability has served as a vivid model for the ministry Catherine and I have shared as teachers and dormitory parents to missionary children. I often wondered why I couldn't say "no" to that one more kid. I don't remember Dad saying, "No I can't . . ."; he was available.

My mother and father were committed to the work of spreading the gospel. In this regard they probably worked as hard as anyone I have ever known. But amid the clutter and busyness of metropolitan New York life and afterward in Florida, Illinois, and Tennessee, they carried out a family practice called "King's day" and "Queen's day." True, while circumstances at times simply did not allow for it, however, the intent and principle have always been of far greater importance to me than the practice of the principle. For the idea itself bespeaks the attitude by which my father approached his marriage and his mate: an attitude of love exemplified in respect, concern, adoration, leadership, comfort, appreciation, devotion, and equality. The King's day was always Sunday, as that was the day of the King of our lives, a day of worship and celebration. The

26

Queen's day was Monday and it was a day for family, but most importantly, it was a day to rekindle the flame of love, to keep the relationship fresh, loving, and actively growing. Depending upon the requirements of the day and the week ahead, this day may have been spent playing a round of golf together—just the two of them—or perhaps simply taking a walk around the block or eating a quiet meal together. Regardless, this practice served as a model of love and of the necessity to cultivate love, to continue the weaving of the tapestry of a marriage, and not simply to sit back idly under the false assumption that a marriage just happens.

My father also portrayed the commodities of independence and individuality. For the sake of clear communication I must contrast individuality with the concept of individualism. As family members we were encouraged to develop our own individuality, to be our own persons with our own personality. People have asked me what it was like to be the son of Stephen Olford. I have never sensed an obligation to be a clone of my father. God has not given me the same gifts that He bestowed upon my dad, and thus I am not a preacher. I am a different person, with different skills, desires, and aspirations and with my own unique approaches. Stephen Olford represented this uniqueness both as a "professional" and as our dad. As a pastor, there was no room for compromise. He was and is a servant of God who has sensed the call to the ministry and has unswervingly followed that course. His direction has come from God in the same way that each of us who are committed to the leading of the Holy Spirit receives divine direction through prayer, the reading of Scripture, circumstance, wise counsel, our own unique skills and personality, and that "still, small voice." He is an individual set apart for a task. Yet he would not espouse individualism, for our insistence on autonomy has caused fragmentation within the body of Christ. My father is a churchman who believes in the community of believers. He is a family man. We are independent and individually responsible before the Lord, but we are not intended to be individualistic and to build walls, but rather to remove them. The ministry of Stephen Olford, Calvary Baptist Church, and Encounter Ministries, in accordance with the principles of his personal and family life, has intended to build believers, not to separate them. Its ministry and lifestyle has had a similar effect on his family and constituency alike, in that it has maintained a strong sense of family loyalty and love, and has united brethren from different denominational and even doctrinal

27

stances. A similar purpose rings throughout all, and this has been the rallying cry of Stephen F. Olford's ministry: "We preach Christ crucified, risen, and coming again."

As this volume celebrates the life and ministry of Stephen Frederick Olford, it is my wish and desire for this tribute to focus our thinking on the man. As my mother and father continue in active ministry, as I look back at their years of shared service, parenthood, and now even in "grandparenthood," I take this opportunity to congratulate them. However, the reason for my congratulation is not that of the thousands who have been touched by the ministry, for there are others making contributions in this volume to signify that. My thanks and indebtedness are expressed because my father and mother taught me to love. They taught me the value of family, fatherhood, motherhood, and a respect for life and love, whether the love is for one's family and friends or the Lord Jesus Christ Himself. When one is born into the family of a public figure, I believe one tends to look beyond the public view. My father was and is real to me, for he has effectively preached what he practiced and practiced what he preached.

NOTE

Reflections of a Son

In this brief tribute to my father, I want to share three very simple epi-
sodes from his life. Each scene is a part of my life, too, and a part of my
relationship with my father. There is a common element to these experiences, and that common element is tears, specifically my father's tears.
My reason for sharing these memories, besides the fact that they are dear
to me, is that they reveal, in part, my father's heart.

The first recollection takes me back to our years at Calvary Baptist
Church in New York City. We were living on the fourteenth floor of the
Hotel Salisbury, directly above Calvary Baptist Church. One afternoon
my father and I were lying on the bed listening to his sermon on the
Encounter radio broadcast. I have forgotten the details of the message.
But I do remember that, at one point in the sermon, my father was speaking about the joy in heaven over the salvation of one lost sinner. He may
have been referring to Luke 15 since verses seven and ten contain this
truth. I'm not sure if I heard something or if I sensed something or if I just
turned and looked at him, but I distinctly remember seeing tears in my
father's eyes. Indeed, he was touched by the very truth that he heard himself preaching. How precious it is to think that heaven itself is filled with
joy over the salvation of one soul who repents!

I would like to make two personal observations about my father in light
of this very simple event. First of all, my father's heart is touched by the
message he preaches. He believes and feels the message he proclaims. In
his own lectures on "incarnational preaching" he teaches that the truth
the preacher proclaims must be fleshed out through his personality. In a
very real sense, the Word must become flesh (see John 1:14). The
preacher must apply the truth to his own life before preaching it. He must
be "real." I wouldn't have expressed all these things about preaching at
the time, but I was learning, in a very deep sense, that my dad meant what
he said. And, indeed, I would come to see that Dad's heart was in his
message, and his message was from his heart.

Secondly, the thought of heaven rejoicing over the repentance of one

29

sinner brought tears to my father's eyes because it touched a responsive chord in his heart as an evangelist. What a joy, what a thrill, what a delight to know that a soul was being saved, someone was being born again, an individual was becoming a child of God! My father has not lost concern for the salvation of people in the busyness of ministry. One of the greatest thrills in his life is to see people respond to the gospel and to the truth of God's Word. My father is a reaper by gift, and he has a reaper's heart. He has always called for a decision, a verdict. Countless times I have listened as he has shared joyfully how people responded to the preaching of the Word. This joy has come from knowing that God has broken through, bringing life and victory into people's lives, and knowing that by God's grace he had a part in what God was doing. My father has never forgotten that response must be of God and through God, nor has he lost confidence in the Word of God to be effective. At the same time he has never lost the sense of responsibility as a preacher to call for response, and he has always experienced great joy when seeing or sensing that people are indeed responding in faith and obedience to the declared Word of God.

The next episode I want to share with you was second in chronological order, but not second in importance. Our family was leaving New York's Kennedy Airport. Mom, Dad, and I had just said goodbye to my brother, Jonathan, and his wife, Catherine, who were on their way to Kijabe, Kenya, for their first term of missionary service at the Rift Valley Academy. From the rear of the car, I saw tears in my father's eyes as he looked across to my mother, who was driving. I'm sure that my mother felt the emotion of the moment, but she had to keep her eyes on the road, while my father looked across to her.

As I reflect on this scene, I think that it represents more than a tender moment. It represents a heart given to family. The tears on that summer day were not tears of disappointment. They were tears of sadness due to the sense of separation that the occasion represented. They were tears of heartache, despite the joy of knowing that a son was serving the Lord. Behind those tears there were years—years of rearing, years of nurturing, and years of an availability that still continue. Behind those tears there were years of family. My father's heart is for his family, and his family is in his heart.

Further reflection upon this airport scene brings me to comment concerning my father's relationship with his wife. In those quiet, tender moments in the car, I am sure that a lot was being shared. My parents had inscribed on their wedding rings the phrase "together with God," and indeed togetherness has been a hallmark of their relationship. Whether in ministry, crusades, playing golf, shopping, or dining, there has been a companionship, a togetherness that has confirmed that wedding-ring inscription. Although the ministry has at times called for travel and separation, in the deepest sense Dad and Mom are inseparable. And the experiences they have had, such as this goodbye, have been shared experiences. As far as my father is concerned, his heart is with his wife, and his wife is in his heart.

The last episode I want to share may seem very simple, yet it speaks volumes to me. We were living in Wheaton, Illinois, at the time, in a nineteenth-floor apartment. The television was on, and my father and I were watching a gifted minister. I believe he was from Washington, D.C. My father thoroughly enjoyed the preacher and so revelled in the message that it brought tears to his eyes.

This scene, first of all, speaks of my father's love of preaching. He is truly called, motivated, and gifted in preaching the Word of God. He values preaching so greatly, in fact, that he is now seeking to train men in the art of preaching. He has never lost a sense of joy in preaching, both in his own ministry and in listening to others. My father enjoys hearing the Word preached accurately and authoritatively. He enjoys hearing the Word preached with passion and excellence. Although my father would be the first to say that good style or rhetorical ability does not replace the Holy Spirit, he enjoys "the art" of good preaching.

My father's own preaching is filled with fervor and freshness. I would venture to say that, after hearing one of his messages, very few would think it routine, dull, or lifeless. When I reflect on how my father can give himself in preaching, knowing that he often steps into the pulpit with other pressures and responsibilities on him, I appreciate his preaching ministry all the more. My father preaches with passion, and he has a passion for preaching.

There is more to the last scene I described than the love of preaching. My father is a person with a great capacity to enjoy, indeed, to be touched by life. Whether it be the powerful rhetoric of a particular preacher, a beautiful piano concerto, a fantastic shot to the green in golf, or breathtaking scenery, my father has always enjoyed (not endured) such experiences. I admire this quality greatly. It is a wonderful thing to be touched 31 by beauty, excellence, that which is lovely and of good report. But while my father enjoys life he can also be touched with pathos. He does not only have the capacity to enjoy, but also to be moved and to weep. Because of this quality, my father has been able to enter into the worlds of others and appreciate their experiences, interests, and gifts. People who know him at a distance may not know this aspect of his life, which is very special to me.

These three scenes from the past have been in my mind for a long time as I have considered this volume. They have been important to me in my own knowledge, love, and admiration of my father.

I share these reflections in tribute to my father, a man of integrity, loyalty, and fervency—a man with a great heart.

Stephen F. Olford—as a Preacher

W. IAN BARCLAY

For over twenty-five years of ministry I have had a Latin text on my desk: "VERITAS PLATEAT, VERITAS PLACEAT, VERITAS MOVEAT," which means "Make truth plain, make truth interesting, make truth moving." I don't know anyone who fulfills that text more completely than Stephen F. Olford. Robert Chalmers said, "My preaching is a failure if it can charm but not change."[1] Without any doubt, Stephen Olford's preaching is successful in that it both charms and changes. It holds our attention and then makes us capitulate to the truth.

Make Truth Plain

Lord Eccles, in his autobiography *Half-way to Faith,*[2] tells of a church built in a once prosperous sheep farming area of England. Over the years, as farming changed and wool was no longer produced, the population moved away to look for work. The few remaining people found the up-keep of the church difficult and expensive. Major repairs were necessary, but funds were not available. When villagers realized they had a twelfth century crucifix in their possession, they sent it to London to be appraised, hoping it would raise the necessary capital sum. The crucifix had been important in the life of the village, and every year it had been given a new coat of paint in preparation for Easter. The art historian in London began to remove the layers of paint from one of the hands and was quite amazed at the life and vitality of the original carving.

That is what Stephen Olford does in his preaching; he lays bare the truth so that the life and vitality of God's Word can be seen. He exposes the truth so that there is no doubt about its meaning. Dr. Billy Graham, from the beginning of his ministry, has frequently declared, *"the Bible says . . . ."* Stephen Olford does not reiterate that phrase, but the result is just as explicit. When listening to him there is no doubt about the meaning 33 of a particular passage, the personal demands that it makes, and exactly what the hearers should do.

I first met Dr. Olford at the Keswick Convention in Barbados in the early 1970s. It was one of those extraordinary occasions when two preachers say similar things and preach from almost identical passages. On the opening evening, while Dr. Olford was still arriving and passing through the West Indian immigration and customs, I preached from the first psalm, speaking on a beatitude from the Old Testament. The next morning of the convention, Dr. Olford announced he was going to speak on the beatitudes from the Sermon on the Mount. People who attended the Keswick Convention that year thought the preachers were consulting each other on what to say. But there was no collusion, simply the prompting of the Holy Spirit. It was a memorable occasion for me, and I have never ceased to enjoy working with Dr. Olford in various parts of the world.

Make Truth Interesting

The preacher's function is not only to hold the crowd: he must also seek to arrest them with the truth. Augustine said, "So ought the preacher to fulfill his task that he teaches, attracts and turns."[3] Here Augustine is stating the three clear divisions that are in the little Latin text on my desk. I know many able expositors who can reveal the clear meaning of Scripture, and I know many interesting preachers. But I know no Bible teacher who has the true gift of the evangelist to move people in obedience to the Word in the way that Dr. Olford does. I have been with him at large pastors' meetings where literally thousands have responded to his preaching and have gone forward for recommitment. If I were asked to say which part of Stephen Olford's preaching I feel is the most unique, I would have to say it is this ability to move people in response to the Word.

Stephen Olford is a man blessed by God with many gifts, and he treats each one of them as God-given, using them in a humble, powerful way. I believe that future generations will look back at his ability to make people respond to the Word of God.

NOTES

1. John Wood, *The Preacher's Workshop* (London: Tyndale Press, 1965), p. 19.
2. David McAdam Eccles, *Half-way to Faith* (Philadelphia: Westminster Press, 1966).
3. Wood, p. 13.

Part 2:
Preaching: God's Method

The Infallible Word of God

W. A. CRISWELL

For the prophecy came not in old time by the will of man; but holy men of God spake as they were moved by the Holy Ghost (2 Peter 1:21, KJV).

From a thoughtful reading of 2 Peter 1:21 and the preceding verses, 15 through 20, a remarkable fact becomes obvious. It is the paramount place that the Bible, God's Word, "the . . . sure word of prophecy," has in the apostle's thinking as being "more sure," more reliable in attesting "the power and coming of Jesus Christ" than the personal experiences which the disciples themselves had with the Lord during His earthly ministry.

Simon Peter, the chief apostle, had said that he knew the time of his own departure was at hand. He had come to that hour when he was soon to "put off this my tabernacle." His decease was not long to be postponed. But to his readers he said in effect, "I shall endeavor to write down these things concerning the deity of our Lord before I am taken from you." He is referring to the gospel of Mark. "For," he says, and I paraphrase, "we have not followed cunningly devised fables. We have not delivered to you myths and legends concerning the heavenly life and miraculous ministry of Jesus our Lord. For we saw those things with our eyes and we heard those things with our ears. Yes," he says, "we even heard the voice of the Father God in heaven saying, 'This is my beloved Son in whom I am well pleased.'" And then he adds this astonishing thing: "But we have a more sure word of prophecy (the Word of God, the Bible)."

This statement is astonishing because he had just said (and again I paraphrase), "I am going to write down these things that I have seen with my eyes and I have heard with my ears, even the voice of the Father in heaven authenticating the ministry of the Divine Son." But now he writes that the surest word of verification for the marvelous, miraculous ministry of the Lord Jesus is not the voice of the Father from heaven. It is not the things

37

the apostles witnessed having seen them with their own eyes, nor the things they wrote down having heard them with their own ears. But the surest verification for Christ's ministry is the "more sure word of prophecy." That is almost unbelievable but that is what Peter writes.

Then he describes that sure word of prophecy. "For (the sure word of) prophecy came not in old time by the will of man." Man did not think it up, nor was it human genius that wrote it down. It is not Shakespearean or Miltonian or Homeric genius or inspiration. But holy men of God spoke as they were moved by the Holy Ghost. Now that is the biblical idea of the inspired Word of God. Holy men of God wrote it down, they spoke, used words and syllables, sentences and paragraphs, language, ideas and thoughts. They wrote as they were moved by the Holy Spirit of God.

How different is the modern, popularly accepted idea of the writing of the holy Scriptures! I shall quote from an eminent theologian who is apologizing for the Bible, and in quoting his testimony, I am giving you the attitude of almost the entire modern theological world. He is not unique in his views; he is just expressing the persuasion of the majority of contemporary theologians. As he apologizes for the Bible, he says: "Of course, there are scientific errors in the Bible. However, we can excuse such mistakes on the grounds that the Bible is not a textbook of science and therefore we do not expect it to be scientifically accurate."

I agree with the theologian on one thing, that the Bible is not a textbook on science. The Bible is the Word of God written for the salvation of our souls that we might be delivered from damnation and hell. If a man ever sees the face of God, if a man ever goes to heaven, he must go by the revelation and truth imparted to us in the holy Word of God. There is no other way to be saved. "There is none other name under heaven given among men whereby we must be saved." There is only one way to be saved and that way is revealed in the sacred Book. We are not to read the Bible as a textbook on civics, geometry, astronomy, cosmogony or anthropology. It is a book of God to show us how to be saved. I agree, therefore, that it is not a textbook on science.

The rest of the statement is blasphemy: "Of course, there are scientific errors in the Bible. However, we can excuse such mistakes . . . we do not expect it to be scientifically accurate." My brother, if the Bible is not also scientifically accurate it is not, to me at least, the Word of God. I have a very plain reason for that. The Lord God who made this world and all the

scientific marvels which we are now discovering in it—that same Lord

God knew all these things from the beginning. We do not surprise Him with our discovery of the waves on which our church services are broadcast and televised. God made those waves in the beginning and we have just discovered them. Jet propulsion that speeds planes along through the sky is not a surprise to God. He made that force in the beginning. Now if the Bible is the Word of God, and if God inspired it, then it cannot contain any scientific mistakes because God knew every truth and fact of science from the beginning.

When we compare the Word of God with science, much of which is actually hypothetical, theoretical guesswork by men who are mostly darkened in counsel; when we come to compare the Bible with these modern pseudo-scientific theories and postulates and hypotheses, let us be careful of two things. First, let us be very certain that we are conversant with the Word of God. Let us be sure that we know the Word of God when we start thinking about the scientific facts that apparently contradict the Bible.

Some time ago there was a world-famous minister who was also a scientist, who loved both God and His marvelous works. From one side of this nation to the other, he published in all the newspapers an advertisement saying that he would give $1,000 to anyone, anywhere, anytime who could point out to him one scientific error in the Bible. He received a letter, among others, from a graduate of the University of Michigan who resided in Detroit. She was claiming that $1,000 for, she declared, she had found a certain scientific error in the Bible. It is said to be true, she pointed out, that the Garden of Eden was in the Valley of Mesopotamia. (That is correct because the Euphrates River ran through it.) But she added, "It has been scientifically demonstrated that no apples can grow in the Mesopotamian Valley, and we are told in the Bible that Adam and Eve were driven out of the Garden of Eden because they ate of the fruit of an apple tree. Therefore," she said, "I am waiting for my $1,000."

The minister wrote back to her, "My dear, the Bible mentions the fruit of the tree of the knowledge of good and evil; it does not mention an apple." The woman finally wrote back, after thorough investigation, and said, "I can not find in the Bible where it says *apple,* but I know it is there because my teacher told me so."

Let me tell you something I found this week. Reading in preparation for this sermon, I stumbled across the debate concerning the adoption of the Gregorian calendar. That is the calendar that we live by now. It is the calendar that has been adopted by all of the civilized world. As you know, 39

January 1 begins our New Year in the Gregorian calendar. Did you know that when the Gregorian calendar was adopted and men were discussing it and debating it, its beginning date, January 1, was bitterly opposed on the ground that Eve ate an apple and apples do not ripen until September? Therefore, they argued, the year began in the Bible in September—all on the basis of Eve's eating an apple in the fall of the year!

I am just saying that first, we must be sure and certain that we are conversant with the Word of God and what it says.

Second, let us be sure of our scientific facts. True science is always changing. It is like a chicken, always moulting. Did you know that it has been estimated that in the library of the Louvre in Paris, France, there are at least three and one-half miles of books on science which are obsolete, outdated, outmoded, so that nobody ever reads a syllable of them anymore? A book of science ten years old is nine years obsolete. Just think of that!

Now, what if you were to take this Bible and update it to the latest scientific fads and theories and hypotheses? Think of what you would do to the Bible. Think of what you would have done to the Bible in 1000 B.C. had you updated it then to the latest scientific fad. What would you have done to the Bible in 500 B.C.? What would you have done in A.D. 1? What would you have done in A.D. 500? What would you have done in A.D. 1000? What would have become of the Bible had you put into it all the scientific ideas and conjurations and monstrosities of A.D. 1660? You would have had a new edition in 1760 and another one in 1860. And had we done so in 1960 we should be looking for a new edition in 1970. Had you updated the Bible according to the latest scientific fads in any generation, in fact, it would have been filled with pseudo-scientific absurdities and nonentities.

Did you know that in 1861 the French Academy of Science published a little brochure in which they stated fifty-one scientific facts that controverted the Word of God? Today there is not a scientist in the world who believes a single one of those fifty-one so-called scientific facts that in 1861 were published as controverting the Word of God. Not one!

The most phenomenal thing of all this is that the Bible, the Word of God, has not changed. Every syllable of it is just as it was when God, through the Holy Spirit, wrote it down. The Bible was written by forty authors over a period of one thousand and five hundred years. Most of them did not know each other personally. There was no collaboration, no collusion. And they wrote, each one of them, as they were inspired of the Holy Spirit of God, over a period of one thousand and five hundred years. Yet with all of the unbelievable, weird, wild background of the days in which they lived there is no repercussion of any of that darkness and superstition in the Word of God.

For instance, in Acts 7:22, we are told that Moses was learned in all of the science of the Egyptians. Moses was learned in all of the wisdom—all the *sophia*—of the Egyptians. He knew all the latest scientific fads, he was abreast with all of the latest scientific discoveries in his day.

Now we can know exactly what Moses was taught. Archaeologists have dug up and put together all of these things that Moses read, all the textbooks of science in his day. They are now before us and we can study them just as Moses did in his day. Those Egyptians were brilliant people. They had a science of cosmogony, the origination of the world, the creation of the world. Those Egyptian scientists believed in Moses' day that this earth was hatched out of a great cosmic egg, an egg that had wings and was flying around through space. According to the latest Egyptian scientific facts, as this enormous winged egg flew around, the processes of mitosis on the inside of the shell were completed and out hatched the world. Out of that flying ovum, here we are! That was the latest scientific theory among those who taught in the days of Moses.

So I turn over here to the Word of God expecting to read about that flying egg, for after all, Moses was learned in all the science of the Egyptians. But I find nothing at all about that enormous hatchery. Instead of that, I read of creation in the sublimest words that man could pen: "In the beginning God created the heavens and the earth."

Those Egyptians also had a science of astronomy. They believed that the sun was the reflection of the light on the earth, and that the earth was the center of this universe. But in Genesis I find that Moses reversed the order—it is the sun that gives light to the earth.

The Egyptians had a science of anthropology. They were naive evolutionists. They believed that mankind sprang from little white worms that they found in the slime and ooze and mud of the alluvial deposit after the Nile's annual overflow. Perhaps they supposed so because they had observed the metamorphosis of a caterpillar into a butterfly. The scientists of Moses' day with their theory of evolution from worms were not far behind those today who would have you believe that your remote ancestors were flea-bitten apes hanging by their tails in a primeval jungle. I read 41 in the Bible that Moses was learned in all the science of the Egyptians. But he says nothing about those little white worms and how we were descended from them. Instead he writes in the most majestic language in human speech: "And God said, Let us make man in our image, after our likeness . . . So God created man in His own image, in the image of God created He him; male and female created He them."

The Bible is thus throughout the whole Word of God. It does not reflect the scientific background of the day in which it was written. The Bible is a historical book but it has been kept from error by the Holy Spirit of God.

In the background of many of the centuries of the Bible is the Chaldean civilization. They also had definite scientific hypotheses concerning the origin of the world and all things therein. Their cosmogony went like this: the earth is one gigantic monster, covered with feathers and scales. The feathers and the scales are the rocks and the trees. As a flea lives in the hair of the hide of a dog, so the human race lives on the hide of this big monster and we burrow into the rocks and live beneath the trees. Then, they said, if you dig down too far and hurt that monster, he will shake himself and buildings will fall down. They had scientific proof for their theory. For they did dig down into the earth (for such things as gold and silver), and earthquakes did happen and buildings did fall down. Such was their scientific proof for their theory of what kind of a world we live in. But in all of the Word of God you will not find a semblance of that monstrous weirdness.

Consider the Babylonian people. Much of the Bible is written against the cultural and scientific background of their civilization. The Babylonians also had a theory of anthropology, of human creation. They said that in the beginning there was a monster by the name of Tia-mat and a great god by the name of Marduk. These two had a fierce battle and Marduk overcame Tia-mat. When Marduk flattened out Tia-mat, his body became the earth. Then, according to the latest Babylonian science of those days, Marduk spit and where he spat men came up, much like the dragonseed that Jason sowed. And then the men spat, and wherever the men spat women came up. And then the women spat, and wherever the women spat animals came up. That was the latest scientific theory in Babylonian days. Do you find any of that idiocy in the Word of God? Yet all of such mythology and a thousand other things just as wild and weird and unimaginable were currently believed in the days when the Bible was written. Such was the science of that day.

Let us turn now to the Word of God to see what kind of scientific background is written here large upon the pages of God's holy Book. Choosing from a multitude of passages, let us turn first to Job 26:7: "God stretcheth out the north over the empty places and hangeth the earth upon nothing." Look at that north star up there in the universe of God shining alone! "And God hangeth the earth upon nothing." Did you know that human beings, for thousands of generations before and after Job wrote these scientific words, believed that the earth was sustained by some kind of solid foundation? Everyone did. Every civilization did. Every culture did. Every nation did.

The Egyptians said that the world is sustained by five great pillars, one at each corner and one in the middle. Five great pillars, they said, sustained the earth. When Job wrote, "God hangeth the world upon nothing," that was not the science of the Egyptians. The Greeks were taught to believe that this world is held up by an immense giant by the name of Atlas, upon whose great shoulders and back the world rested. That is what the learned, sophisticated Greeks believed. The Hindu scientist and theologian believed that this earth is sustained on the back of a gigantic elephant, that the elephant stands on the back of an enormous sea-turtle, and that the sea-turtle swims in a cosmic ocean. Then he ran out of imagination and quit without saying what the ocean stands on. But that was their latest scientific theory in the day Job wrote, "God hangeth the earth on nothing."

Turn now to Isaiah 11:12: "And he (God) shall set up an ensign for the nations, and shall assemble the outcasts of Israel, and gather together the dispersed of Judah from the four corners of the earth." All the infidels and cynics and critics and new lights in theology say, "See, look what Isaiah wrote: 'God shall gather the dispersed of Judah from the four corners of the earth.' Therefore, in keeping with the scientific theories of his day, Isaiah believed the earth was flat and that it had four corners." This is one of the passages they quote to criticize.

Remembering that Isaiah wrote not in English but in Hebrew, and that to know what Isaiah said one must read the original Hebrew text, I looked it up. His Hebrew idiom is altogether different from our English idiom but both mean the same thing. We say "the four corners of the earth" meaning the whole world. For example, during a violent storm at sea when the passengers on the boat became afraid, the captain called them all together and said: "Now you listen to me. I have sailed this boat to the 43 four corners of the seas and I tell you this wind is not dangerous. This is just a hard blow." Another example comes from signs the United States government placed in all the post offices, reading, "Join the United States Marines and visit the four corners of the earth."

Isaiah presents the same meaning in Hebrew. The Hebrew idiom meaning "to the farthest extremity" is taken from the spreading of a bird's wings. The Hebrew word for the two wings of a bird is *kenepoth*. Isaiah says in Hebrew idiom, "And he shall gather together the dispersed of Judah from the four *kenepoth* of the earth—from the four *wings* of the earth." Thus I discovered why the Hebrew used the idiom *wings* to refer to the uttermost parts of the earth. It was their word for "extremity." When a bird spread out its wings, there was an extremity accurately described. That is as far as the extremity would stretch. The prophet could have said, "from the four parts of the compass—north, south, east and west—God is going to gather His children together." But he more graphically said it the other way.

Now it is just such discrepancies in translations that seem baffling. But if you know your Bible you will not be confused by the critics. These so-called scientific errors in the Bible melt away under close analysis.

Turn to Isaiah 40:22: "It is he that sitteth upon the circle of the earth." When Isaiah wrote that, there was not a living man in the world who believed that the world was round. Not one. Isaiah lived around 750 B.C. and there was not a man in the earth before him nor after him for countless generations, who believed that the earth was round. But look what Isaiah wrote by the Spirit of God: "He that sitteth upon the circle of the earth."

Let us turn again to 1 Corinthians 15:39: "All flesh is not the same flesh: but there is one kind of flesh of men, another flesh of beasts, another of fishes, and another of birds." We could translate the passage like this: "All protoplasm is not the same protoplasm. There is one protoplasm of men, there is another protoplasm of beasts, there is another protoplasm of fishes, there is another protoplasm of birds." That is what Paul wrote.

But when men discovered cells, and when on the inside of cells they discovered protoplasm, it became the scientific rage to avow that all life was made out of the same and identical stuff—protoplasm. But Paul wrote that that was not so. He wrote that there is a protoplasm of men and that the protoplasm of men is not like the protoplasm of animals; and the pro-

toplasm of animals is not like the protoplasm of fishes; and the protoplasm of fishes is not like the protoplasm of birds. After we became more
learned and our scientists finally discovered the truth, we found it to be
exactly as Paul wrote. The cytoplasm and the nuclei on the inside of the
cells of a man are altogether different from the cytoplasm and the nuclei
on the inside of the cells of any other animal or beast or bird, and all of
them are different from one another. Isn't that remarkable?

Turn to Hebrews 1:10-12, which quotes from Psalm 102:25-27:
"Thou, Lord, in the beginning hast laid the foundation of the earth; and
the heavens are the works of thine hands. They shall perish; but thou
remainest; and they all shall wax old as doth a garment; And as a vesture
shalt thou fold them up, and they shall be changed: but thou art the same,
and thy years shall not fail."

Did you know that here is a better scientific statement of Sir James
Jeans' book, *The Wider Aspects of Cosmology* than Jeans himself wrote?
For he finally came to the conclusion that this universe is like a great
clock that is running down, running down. Every time there is liberation
of energy, the complex molecular structure of a substance dissolves,
breaking down into simpler construction. But you can never put that
energy back into it again and you can never build it up again. This whole
universe is like a vast wound-up clock. It is running down, running down,
running down, and finally someday even the sun will go out and this universe will be extinct.

"Thou, Lord, (made the heavens and the earth) in the beginning (God
wound it up) . . . They shall perish; but thou remainest; and they all shall
wax old as doth a garment; And as a vesture shalt thou fold them up, and
they shall be changed (they shall die): but thou art the same, and thy years
shall not fail."

The latest scientific theories are confirmed by the Word of God. To take
just one other example, turn to Hebrews 11:3: "Through faith we understand that the worlds were framed by the word of God, so that things
which are seen were not made of the things which do appear." Let me
paraphrase that: "So that the things that are visible are made out of entities that are invisible." Did you ever hear a finer statement of the molecular, atomic, nature of this universe in substance and reality than that?
"The things that are visible, the things that we see, are made out of things,
entities, that are invisible, made out of things you cannot see."

From beginning to end there is not a word or a syllable or a revelation 45 in the Word of God that has contradicted or ever will contradict any true, substantiated scientific fact. The reason is very simple. The Lord God who inspired the Book is the Lord God who made these things from the beginning. That is why when the Lord speaks through His servants, you can base your life and your soul and your salvation on what God has said.

There is not a more familiar story in the annals of literature than the story that describes the death of the immortal Scottish poet and novelist, Sir Walter Scott. As he lay dying he turned to his son-in-law, Lockhart, and said to him, "Son, bring me the Book." There was a vast library in Walter Scott's home and, bewildered, the son-in-law said, "Sir, what book? Which book?" The dying bard replied, "My son, there is just one Book. Bring me *the* Book." It was then that Lockhart went to the library and brought to Sir Walter Scott the Bible.

"For the prophecy came not . . . by the will of man: but holy men of God spake as they were moved by the Holy Ghost" (2 Peter 1:21). And this is the inerrant, infallible, holy, eternal Word of the living God. "The grass withereth, the flower fadeth; but the Word of our God shall stand for ever" (Isa. 40:8). "Heaven and earth will pass away, but my word will not pass away" (Mark 13:31). "For ever, O Lord, thy word is firmly fixed in the heavens" (Ps. 119:89, RSV). Oh, what a blessedness, what a holiness, what a foundation, eternal and immovable, is the living Word of the living God! "And his name is called The Word of God" (Rev. 19:13).

NOTES

Unabridged essay originally published in *The Bible for Today's World* by W. A. Criswell (Grand Rapids, Mich.: Zondervan Publishing House, 1965).
Scripture quotations in this article are from the KING JAMES VERSION of the Bible.

Inerrancy:
The Issue Is Settled

W. L. PROBASCO

Jesus answered them, "Is it not written in your law, 'I said, "You are gods"'? If He called them gods, to whom the word of God came (and the Scripture cannot be broken), do you say of Him whom the Father sanctified and sent into the world, 'You are blaspheming,' because I said, 'I am the Son of God'?

"If I do not do the works of My Father, do not believe Me; but if I do, though you do not believe Me, believe the works, that you may know and believe that the Father is in Me, and I in Him" (John 10:34–38, NKJV).

We can stop arguing. The issue of inerrancy has been settled. If Jesus Christ is God incarnate as He claimed to be, then inerrancy is a matter of fact because He affirmed it. If He is not, then Southern Baptists and all other Christians have an infinitely greater problem to deal with, since our faith is vain and meaningless if Jesus is not "God with us."

The primary issue to be considered in our battle for the Bible is not the inerrancy of Scripture, but the deity of Jesus Christ. He declared Himself to be the eternal Son of God and claimed that Scripture is absolutely authoritative. What is more, the Scripture that He claimed "cannot be broken" was the Scripture of His own day, not the original autographs. We have the authority of the One Who claimed to be God, speaking for the authority of the Word that claims to be from God. We have the word of the Eternal Word about the written Word. These two issues, the one primary (the deity of Christ) and the other secondary (the inerrancy of Scripture), converge in John 10:22–39.

Before attempting an exposition of this passage, I should remind you that the argument among Southern Baptists over inerrancy centers in the autographs of the Old and New Testaments. Since we do not possess them, some of us believe that we can never say the Bible is inerrant. How, 47 they argue, could we possibly know for sure that every word is inspired? The point I hope to underscore from this passage is that it makes no difference whether or not we have the autographs. We can trust our Bible to carry the same authority as the originals because we have God's statements to that effect. If He is God, then we have no basis for doubting anything He says, including His affirmations regarding the integrity of Scripture.

It is likely that the majority of Southern Baptists believe in what I will call total inerrancy: that every word of the Bible is inspired by God and is true in all matters about which it speaks. I would agree that inerrancy can be affirmed only for the original autographs, but I would also express my profound conviction that our present copies of the Bible carry the same authority as the originals. The ground of that conviction lies in statements made by our Lord, in which He assures us of divine authority for the Bible that He read from, which was at least fourteen hundred years removed from the earliest written Old Testament books.

I chose this passage because of the perspective it gives us on inerrancy. Jesus Christ is claiming deity for Himself and absolute authority for Scripture, all in one context. It was the celebration of the Dedication, or Hanukkah as it is called today. Jewish leaders had raised the issue of His claim to be the Christ (a title that must include deity, if we associate it with the messianic passages of the Old Testament). "How long will you keep us in suspense?" they demanded. "If you are the Christ, tell us plainly" (John 10:24). Out of His answers come two clear assertions: First, Jesus claimed deity for Himself. Second, He pronounced His divine authority in two crucial and interrelated matters—the security of His sheep and the inerrancy of the Scriptures.

Christ Claims His Own Deity

Now and then I hear someone from our ranks make a preposterous statement to the effect that Jesus never claimed to be God. That no doubt delights the Mormons, and followers of "The Way," and other cults. I don't know how much clearer Jesus needs to be in His claim to be the eternal and incarnate Son of God. He declared His deity in two ways, and they are represented in this passage.

First, Jesus declared His deity by His works: "Many good works I have shown you from My Father" (John 10:32). He meant that if he was able to do things that only God could do, then His works should communicate His divine nature. One logically must infer that only a divine person could do divine works. Second, Jesus declared His deity verbally. In verse 30, for instance, He was so bold as to claim, "I and My Father are one." In the Greek, He means "one thing," or "one kind," not "one person." Jesus did not claim to be the same person as God the Father, but equal in substance. In verse 36, it is recorded that ". . . I said I am God's Son." And the Jews understood perfectly what He meant. They called Him a mere man and took up stones to kill Him, an act which indicates that they believed Him to be blaspheming by claiming to be God.

Our Lord's claims of deity are not confined to this passage, however. Who can deny that He used the ineffable name "I AM" many times? This includes the well-known statement in John 8:58, "Before Abraham was, I AM." In his formal defense before the Sanhedrin in Mark 14:61-62, "The high priest asked Him, 'Are you the Christ, the Son of the Blessed One?' And Jesus said, 'I am: and you shall see the Son of man sitting on the right hand of power, and coming in the clouds of heavens.'" At this point the high priest tore his clothes, another extreme expression of contempt. We cannot escape the implications of the Sanhedrin's sentence that Jesus be crucified. He was put on the cross because He claimed to be God incarnate!

Jesus not only declared His deity, He demonstrated it. He said, in verses 37 and 38, "Do not believe Me unless I do what the Father does. But if I do it, even though you do not believe Me, believe the signs that you may learn and understand that the Father is in Me and I am in the Father." The gospel of John is, in fact, built around the thematic selection of seven signs that Jesus did, beginning with the creation of wine out of water and climaxing with the greatest of all signs, the resurrection. In John 2, when the Jews demanded an explanation for His messianic act of cleansing the temple, He replied that His claim would be proven by His death and subsequent resurrection.

Did he literally rise again? There is more evidence for Christ's resurrection than for any other event of classical history, and we do not even have to depend on an infallible or inerrant Bible to have more than reasonable evidence that the resurrection took place as recorded in the Gospels. We simply have to realize that these primary source documents are historiographically sound and reliable and that they pass all three tests that a historian would impose upon a document to determine the genuineness of 49 its records: external tests, internal tests, and textual tests. Applied to the Gospels and Acts, these tests overwhelmingly support the truth of the events recorded in the Gospels and Acts. These books contain eyewitness accounts of those who saw Jesus Christ crucified by experts, pronounced dead by the authorities, placed in a tomb, and on the third day rise again. "He showed Himself alive after His passion with many infallible proofs," says Luke (Acts 1:3). Peter, John, and the others saw Him alive. In fact, John records that they actually heard Him speak, saw Him with their eyes, and actually touched His body. They knew that He was alive and not only recorded what they knew to be true but laid down their lives as testimony to that truth.

We must also remember that God believes the resurrection to have been witnessed sufficiently to make the gospel binding upon everyone. He expects us to believe that Jesus died for our sins according to the Scriptures, was buried, and rose again the third day according to the Scriptures (1 Cor. 15:1–7). We may deny the accuracy or reliability of the eyewitness accounts of Christ's mighty works, but God holds us accountable for the evidence presented by those witnesses. On Mars Hill, Paul stressed this very point. The superstitious Athenians had erected an altar "to the unknown god," but the apostle declared to them that God was not unknown. He is personally available to everyone. He is both known and near. And because God is available, we are accountable. How do we know that God has made Himself known and has drawn near? And how is it that God can therefore demand that we repent of our detestable failure to acknowledge Him? "Because He has appointed a day, in which He will judge the world in righteousness by that Man whom He hath ordained; whereof He hath given assurance (evidence) to all men, in that He hath raised Him from the dead" (Acts 17:31). The fact of the resurrection is enough to make repentance and faith mandatory for every person on earth.

A college professor told me once, as we were discussing the deity of Jesus, "Well, so He rose again. But what does that prove? He might have been a Martian, or just a superhuman with powers we haven't discovered yet." My reply was, "My friend, you don't have as much sense as I thought you did. Anyone who can go into death and come out again under His own power has every right to tell us what His resurrection means. And by His own claim, His resurrection means that He is God in the flesh!"

INERRANCY: THE ISSUE IS SETTLED

Christ Asserts His Divine Authority

If Jesus is God, then He is infinitely qualified to speak with final authority on any issue. He asserts His divine authority in this passage on two crucial issues that arise out of the primary issue of His claim to be the Son of God: the security of His sheep and the inerrancy of Scripture.

The Lord flatly asserts in verses 27–30 that His sheep are securely held in His hand, and they can never be snatched away. This assertion was part of His answer to the Jews who had seen His miracles but refused to accept their implications. Their problem in believing was not due to lack of evidence. It was that such a conviction must be revealed in us by the Spirit. "You do not believe because you are not of My sheep. My sheep hear My voice, and I know them, and they follow Me, and I give unto them eternal life, and they shall never perish. (The Greek text is translated, 'they shall by no means perish unto the age.') Neither shall any one seize them out of My hand. My Father, Who has given them to Me, is greater than all, and no one is able to seize them out of the hand of the Father. I and the Father, We are one" (John 10:26–30).

Why speak of the security of sheep in answer to a question raising the issue of His deity? Because deity carries final, ultimate authority, and one of the greatest tests of Jesus' authority is His ability to keep His own children secure! If sin, death, hell, or the devil can reclaim those whom He redeemed, then He cannot claim to be the Christ.

The security of His sheep is asserted by two facts about them. First, they share in His nature (10:27–28). They are spiritually alive to His word and intimately and inseparably bound to Him like sheep are bound to their shepherd. And they are obediently responsive to His authority. Second, they are saved by His power. Who can escape the implications of Christ's threefold statement, "I give unto them eternal life; and they shall never perish, neither shall any one pluck them out of my hand" (John 10:28). They cannot be plucked out of His hand because if they are in Jesus' hand, they are also in the Father's hand. Jesus and the Father are one. They share the same divine nature and power.

There is a direct relationship between Christ's assertion about His sheep and His assertion about the Scriptures. The Father gave both. He gave the sheep to the Son and the Scriptures to humanity. The sheep cannot ever be snatched away once they are in the Shepherd's hand. The Scriptures cannot ever lose their authority once they are written down. 51

To show that scriptural principle was behind his claim to deity, the Lord quoted an obscure and misunderstood passage from Psalm 82 (NIV). "Is it not written in your Law, he said, 'I said you are gods'?" If He called them "gods" to whom the Word of God came—and the Scriptures cannot be broken—what about the One whom the Father set apart as His very own and sent into the world? "Why then do you accuse me of blasphemy because I said, 'I am God's Son'?" (John 10:36, NIV).

Experts in textual studies tell us that Jesus spoke these words in the form of a syllogism, which is an argument consisting of a major premise, a minor premise, and a conclusion agreeing with both. To illustrate, a major premise would be, "A bank robber is a lawbreaker." A minor premise would be, "Jack is a bank robber." The conclusion agreeing with both would then be, "Therefore, Jack is a lawbreaker."

The major premise in this statement by our Lord is that Scripture cannot be broken. Its authority cannot in any way be diminished by separating one part of it from another or holding one part as less authoritative than another. Even a passage like Psalm 82 is as much the Word of God as one of the great, well-known passages. The minor premise is that in the Scriptures God said to some of the judges of Israel, "You are gods." If one occupies a God-ordained office within the theocracy, he has the very authority of God behind him. He speaks and acts on God's behalf.

The conclusion of this syllogistic statement is inescapable. If Scripture cannot be broken, and if it is true that a fallible human occupying a God-ordained office carries the authority of God and can be called a "god" in that sense, it is certainly scriptural and valid for the incarnate Jesus, Who has come out of heaven and Who has been sanctified as the Christ, to call Himself the Son of God.

The Scripture Cannot Be Broken

Finally, let me concentrate on that major premise, "the Scripture cannot be broken." We cannot ignore the observation that the eternal Son of God has made this assertion about the Scriptures. Nor can we ignore the implications of that assertion. From the authority of His deity, He has stated that the Word of God is fully binding and carries the weight of God's authority, and that the authority of the whole is carried into each part. We cannot say that one passage is authoritative and inerrant, but another is not.

It is astounding that the Lord would choose this particular passage as an example of inerrancy. He unapologetically appeals to the fact that this Scripture, too, "is written in your law" (Old Testament). He therefore accredits the position taken by inerrantists that since the Word of God is given in human language, the Scriptures are verbally inspired. In another well-known statement Jesus affirmed that "One jot or one tittle will in no way pass from the law till all be fulfilled" (Matt. 5:18).

Do you recall the angelic warfare which took place in heaven over the giving of a portion of the Word of God to Daniel? In chapter 10, the prophet had been fasting for three weeks, waiting for God to reveal the rest of His vision of the last days. When the angel finally appeared to Daniel following a breathtaking and awesome vision of the preincarnate Christ, he told Daniel that the "Prince of Persia," Satan, had hindered him from coming for twenty-one days. A war had been fought between this prince and Michael, the archangel. Finally the messenger angel was allowed to continue his journey to earth and to give Daniel this vision for a time yet to come. Why did the devil want to keep the angel of God from delivering that prophecy to Daniel? Because he knew that once it was written down, it could not be changed! God guarantees His Word by having it written down. When it is written, it is as good as done! It cannot be broken!

Couple this with the fact that this is an unusually difficult and little understood passage—one not usually quoted—and you realize that even the most troublesome, ordinary, or unbelievable passages in the Bible are absolutely authoritative. Their message cannot be altered, embellished, or explained away, because they have been written under inspiration from God.

Add to this passage all others that contain our Lord's assertions about the inspiration and authority of the Scriptures and we don't need the originals to know if the Old Testament is inerrant. Jesus made that very pronouncement about the Old Testament of His own day, and it is not likely that any of the autographs were then in existence. In fact, He fully affirmed those Old Testament passages that give us the most trouble—the account of creation and Adam, the account of the great flood, and of Jonah and his experience with the great fish. So much did Jesus trust those passages that He based great doctrines upon them. He built His teaching about marriage upon the account of the creation of the first home with Adam and Eve. The flood was told as fact and was given as the precursor 53 of the judgment yet to come upon the earth. Jonah's salvation from the belly of the fish became identified with the doctrine of Christ's resurrection.

Some will say, "What of the New Testament?" The same divine Lord has spoken with equal authority on that subject as well. In the fourteenth chapter of John, Jesus promised to send the Holy Spirit, and among His ministries was to be the giving of further Scripture: "But the Counselor, the Holy Spirit, whom the Father will send in my name, will teach you all things and will remind you of everything I have said to you" (14:26). He was going to give His apostles total recall of all of Christ's teachings, and He was going to guide them in communicating the truth. This I understand to be Christ's seal of authority upon those writings by the apostles that were later to be received as canonical. By the authority of Christ Himself, we may verify the divine accuracy of the New Testament, along with its full authority, just as we do the Old Testament.

Conclusion: Do We Need the Originals?

I do not believe that we need the original texts to guarantee that our present Bible carries the same authority as the autographs. Once the deity of Christ is established, in light of His historically verifiable resurrection, recorded in the fully reliable primary source documents of the New Testament, all we need to do is to observe what the Incarnate God has said about the Scriptures of the Old and New Testaments. He has said, "The Scripture cannot be broken." When I hear Him say that, I don't need any other argument. If He could do the things that only God could do, and exhibit power over death and hell itself in His death and resurrection, I believe anything He says. We admit that there are a few unresolved problems in our present texts. This in no way should discourage us from affirming the full authority of Scripture in every matter about which it speaks, science as well as salvation. The Lord Himself has set the evidence clearly before us. If we believe His works, then we must believe His words (John 10:37–38). If we believe His words, then we ought to believe His word on the Word. That word is that the Scriptures cannot be broken; that the authority of one part carries the authority of the whole of the Word of God, and vice versa.

The primary issue, then, is the deity of Christ. Once we affirm that He is the Incarnate God, how can we with any logic or conscience deny His assertions about the inspiration and authority of the Bible?

NOTE

Preaching

PAUL B. SMITH

P reaching is the proclamation of an urgent message to one or more people in such a way that it demands a decision of those who listen. It is scripturally valid, practically necessary, and psychologically powerful.

Scripturally Valid

Preaching is not the same as dialogue, debate, discussion, or even teaching. Preaching requires no participation, no interchange of ideas between leader and listeners. I can find no trace of formal debates in the New Testament, but Jesus and His disciples often invited questions and answered them. The apostle Paul used dialogue most effectively wherever he could find people who would talk to him. Although teaching is one of the gifts of the Holy Spirit (1 Cor. 12:28), it is usually distinguished from preaching.

Two basic words used in the New Testament describe preaching. The first, *kerysso,* means to proclaim as a herald. The second, *evangelizomai,* means to bring good news. The first word is concerned with the method involved in preaching and the second with the message.

As a herald, a preacher does not depend upon a response from the audience. It makes no difference whether the hearers agree or disagree. The preacher's mission is to proclaim a message from God to anyone who will listen.

The word *evangelizomai* is also translated by our infinitive "to preach." This word emphasizes that the message of the preacher is good news. The preacher is not merely a man who is able to say something. He is a man who truly has something to say. The most highly trained person in the world will never be a preacher unless he has a message. Our pulpits are plagued with this kind of intellectual dud who subjects people to an hour of wasted time Sunday after Sunday, simply because he has no message.

On the other hand, a man may have very little training, but if he has a vital message he can be a formidable preacher. Dwight L. Moody was such a preacher. His sermons were cluttered with appalling grammatical blunders because of his lack of formal education, but Christian history cannot be written without including his name. Obviously, the most effective preacher is both highly trained and has a vital message.

Basic content of New Testament preaching went through three stages. John the Baptist proclaimed repentance of sin in view of the coming of the Lamb of God. Jesus proclaimed the coming of the kingdom of God. The disciples combined these messages, preaching Christ crucified, risen, the Son of God, and the Lord of all.

For those who want to preach the gospel of the Christian faith, the apostle Paul leaves absolutely no doubt as to what the message must be. "We preach Christ crucified, unto the Jews a stumbling block, and unto the Greeks foolishness" (1 Cor. 1:23 KJV). "If Christ be not risen, then is our preaching vain, and your faith is also vain" (1 Cor. 15:14). "For the Son of God, Jesus Christ, who was preached among you by us" (2 Cor. 1:19). "For we preach not ourselves, but Christ Jesus the Lord" (2 Cor. 4:5).

The message of the New Testament preacher must consist basically of the death, resurrection, deity, and lordship of Jesus Christ. This is the gospel that "is the power of God unto salvation to every one that believeth" (Rom. 1:16 KJV). There may be many other interesting truths to convey, but unless a message contains these minimum requirements, it is not the gospel of the Christian faith.

Practically Necessary

In addition to its biblical validity, preaching is a practical necessity. Technically, any proclamation of the gospel message is preaching, whether it be to an audience of one or ten thousand. However, in our modern world the term is generally applied only where there is a group of people involved.

Some people object to preaching. They may feel that the Christian faith is best transmitted on a one-to-one basis and that preaching to a large crowd of people is neither scriptural nor effective. Certainly, the most effective method of reaching people with any message is "eyeball to eyeball," where one person is so completely sold on his product that he shares it with others. However, this approach does not work in actual practice. I do not know of any major organization that has been able to sell a message solely on a one-to-one basis. No group has managed to produce that many completely dedicated members or salesmen! This is certainly true in the field of politics. Every astute politician knows the inestimable value of shaking hands, kissing babies, and knocking on doors, but no party seems to have enough workers to reach everyone in this way. Therefore, the politicians use every available means of mass media.

The church of Jesus Christ has a bigger job to do than any political party, and it is a mystery to me how any intelligent person can conclude that the mammoth task of reaching the entire world can be done on a one-to-one basis.

Theoretically, all Christians should be active witnesses, but that is simply not the case. Sometimes there is a lack of dedication, but often personal characteristics make it difficult for some Christians to share their faith with others. This leaves the church in the same position as most other organizations—limited to a minority of dedicated salesmen.

If the multitudes are to be reached, we will always need specialists who can communicate with the masses, whether from the pulpit, through television, by radio, or the printed page. But only a person who refused to face the facts of the expanding world population would attempt to dismiss the preacher as a relic of another generation.

To say that the Christian church should be different from every other organization in this respect is sheer nonsense. It is quite obvious from the records that both Jesus and His disciples were not content to limit themselves to personal confrontations but continually took their stand in front of the largest crowds they could gather.

Psychologically Powerful

Only a person who speaks to large crowds will fully understand the forces that motivate people in a huge gathering. There is a crowd psychology that the church cannot afford to neglect. Emotions are aroused, decisions are made, and actions are taken in the charged atmosphere of a crowd that may never be realized in any other setting. It would be foolish for the Christian church to ignore the psychological power that is unleashed by a crowd.

In addition, a crowd has an immediate psychological effect on the speaker. Regardless of the amount of study and preparation, every preacher is familiar with that flash of inspiration that occasionally sets him on fire once he is in the pulpit. His mind suddenly begins to work like a well-oiled machine. His tongue and lips articulate with the clarity of a trumpet. Combinations of words and phrases flash into his soul like a meteor. An idea that he had struggled with for many hours will suddenly crystallize into a single sentence.

There is also psychological power in a full sermon proclaimed without interruption. In *The Rise and Fall of the Third Reich,* William L. Shirer stresses the fantastic power that Adolf Hitler had as a speaker. Some of Hitler's ablest generals were afraid to have a conference with him because it was usually a one-sided affair that allowed no interruptions. The generals had learned from experience that if they listened to him long enough, they would go out absolutely convinced that he was right. Hitler happened to be in a position from which he could present his entire message without discussion, and usually his audiences were deeply influenced. Had they been given the opportunity to interrupt and object during the course of the speech, the final impact might never have been realized.

Certainly there are times when the Christian faith should be discussed and questions asked but there are other times when the preacher must be permitted to complete his thought and develop his theme if his message is to make the impact that it should. There is a force in a completed message that is missing in its component parts.

A Decision

Perhaps most important is that preaching should demand some kind of decision on the part of the hearers. Certainly this was true of the New Testament preachers. When John the Baptist had finished preaching, the people knew that they had to make a decision. Jesus preached for a decision. He insisted that His followers make an unequivocal committal of their lives to the Father.

The Christian faith involves a radical upheaval within the heart and conscience. This upheaval, which is the new birth, cannot be proclaimed or received passively. It necessitates a decision.

59

NOTE

Scripture quotations in this article are from the KING JAMES VERSION of the Bible.

The Primacy of Preaching

I believe in preaching! The Fall of 1987 marked my thirty-seventh year in one pulpit, and for all those years I have considered preaching to be my primary task. I have been greatly encouraged in this commitment by the example of great preachers of the past and of the present. Among the latter have been Dr. Martyn Lloyd-Jones, Dr. John R. W. Stott, and Dr. Stephen F. Olford. The fact that these are all British preachers speaks well of the quality of British preaching and to the fact that British evangelicals tend toward expository preaching, which constitutes, in my judgment, the only true form of preaching!

Expository sermons derive their content from Scripture itself. They borrow their structure and thrust from a specific passage and apply that passage with directness and urgency to contemporary life. What other modes of preaching often lack is biblical content, causing those in the pews to drown in words while thirsting for knowledge. John Stek of Calvin Seminary puts it well: "Preachers who rummage through the Bible to find texts on which to hang topical sermons are often guilty of substituting their word for the biblical Word."[1] This soon results in an unconscious trivializing of preaching.

Proof of this trivializing is found in the widespread biblical illiteracy that exists today. Many people in the average congregation do not know the meaning of terms such as justification by faith, sanctification, the Kingdom of God, the new covenant, or the walk in the Spirit, the flesh, or even faith, love, and peace! Worse yet, because they do not know the biblical meaning of flesh, for instance, they do not know how to recognize it in themselves. The flesh therefore rages in unrestrained destructiveness throughout their thinking and living. Because they know nothing of the nature of the new covenant, they live continually under the legal bondage of the old. Because they do not understand the wisdom of God, they succumb constantly to the pompous pretensions of the wisdom of the world. Because they do not know how to use the shield of faith, they are besieged daily by the fiery darts of the wicked one.

61

What is essential therefore in preaching is, first of all, content! It is what Paul calls "the unsearchable riches of Christ" (Eph. 3:8). In a verse that has meant much to me personally, Paul calls himself and other first-century preachers "stewards of the mysteries of God" (1 Cor. 4:1). He sees himself as entrusted with a fabulous deposit of truth which he must dispense to others. It ought to be the supreme business of a preacher to discharge that responsibility with utter faithfulness. Paul adds, "It is required of a steward that one be found faithful." So he says, he sought always "to declare . . . the whole counsel of God" (Acts 20:27).

I believe that much of the present weakness in preaching is because preachers fail to understand the uniqueness of the gospel message, and its remarkable power to change a congregation, a community, a city, or even a nation. When Paul came to Corinth, as he tells us, he came "in weakness and fear and much trembling" (1 Cor. 2:3). He was, in fact, intimidated by Corinth! He knew these Greek cities well, and the terrible degradation of Corinth frightened and discouraged him. It looked incurable. Sexual depravity, centered in the temple of Aphrodite overlooking the city, was so widespread and popular it seemed impossible to oppose. Paul knew the superstitious fears of the masses in Corinth and was aware of the dishonesty of its politicians, and the shameless injustice of the city courts.

He had often felt the tyranny of Rome in its iron-fisted control of the whole known world. This was especially evident in Corinth with its history of rebellion. Paul saw daily the hopeless despair of the citizenry: half of them slaves to the other half, living in misery and near starvation. Yet, in contrast, he felt Corinth's pride in its beautiful location; the arrogance of its philosophers as heirs of the great thinkers of Greece; the wealth the city's commerce brought; the acclaim it enjoyed as one of the chief cities of the Roman empire. How could he reach it? How could he change it? It looked impenetrable, unassailable!

But then he remembered his message—and his resource! He began to preach, "not with persuasive words of human wisdom, but in demonstration of the Spirit and of power" (1 Cor. 2:4). That demonstration derived from what he describes in some detail in the subsequent verses, as "the wisdom of God." It is also what he terms in chapter four "the mysteries of God." It has several outstanding characteristics of which I now address three.

THE PRIMACY OF PREACHING

The Wisdom of God Is in Sharp Contrast to the World's Wisdom

"Not the wisdom of this age, nor of the rulers of this age, who are coming to nothing" (1 Cor. 2:6). When Paul speaks of the rulers of this age he means more than government officials. The phrase refers to the leaders of thought in any age—the movers and shakers, the mind-benders—not only statesmen, but philosophers, thinkers, scientists, educators. "Coming to nothing" describes their transient character. Their plans and ideas are in a constant flux. They swing from one extreme to another, flowing in cycles of acceptance like fads in fashion. Everyone knows that any science textbook more than ten years old is totally outdated. Economic theories change like the tides, ebbing and flowing with the Dow-Jones averages. Educational policies come in cycles, alternating between extremes of permissiveness and heavy control. Political programs, all promising boundless prosperity, appear every election year. I have now lived through the New Deal, the Fair Deal, the Great Society, Camelot, Peace with Honor, the Camp David process, and Reaganomics, all promising much, but delivering little.

This constant change gives rise to much of the rush and restlessness of modern living. It is all doomed to pass away or is coming to nothing. Perhaps its effect has best been caught by a modern jingle that reads:

> This is the Age of the half-read page
> And the quick hash, and the mad dash
> The bright night, with the nerves tight
> The plane hop, with a brief stop
> The lamp tan in a short span
> The big shot in a good spot
> And the brain strain and the heart pain
> And the catnaps until the spring snaps
> And the fun's done!

In sharp contrast, the Word of God remains unchanged and unchangeable. Always relevant, always up-to-date, always perceptive and penetrating—eternally accurate!

The Truth of God's Wisdom Is Unique and Unrivaled

"We impart a secret and hidden wisdom of God, which God decreed before the ages for our glorification" (1 Cor. 2:7). The paramount glory 63 of the gospel is that there is nothing like it anywhere else. It is without rival, either in the scientific laboratory, in the psychologist's office, or the philosopher's study. It is this factor that constitutes the supreme value of preaching. It simply does what *nothing* else can do! Paul calls this truth the deep things of God, the thoughts of God, spiritual truth, and the mind of Christ!

When Jesus came He fulfilled the Old Testament prophecy that He "would utter things kept secret since the foundation of the world" (Matt. 13:35). He said, "Many prophets and righteous men have desired . . . to hear what you hear, and did not hear it" (Matt. 13:17). In 1 Corinthians 2:10 Paul declares these truths have now been revealed to us through the Spirit, "[who] searches all things, yes, the deep things of God." Since I preach in a university community, this has always meant to me that when I open the Bible on Sunday morning, I am offering to the physicists, the scientists, the high-tech engineers, the doctors, lawyers, bankers, and captains of industry present, as well as artisans, secretaries, plumbers, and many others essential knowledge about themselves and about life, which they could never learn in any secular college or graduate school! I am privileged to give them an understanding of reality unavailable from any other source.

It is the business of preaching to change the total world view of every member of the congregation; to dispel the secular illusions which abound, and to identify and underscore the concepts and practices that are right. Perhaps the most amazing statement of all in this amazing verse is that this hidden truth is "for *our* glorification!" The Westminster Catechism properly states, "Man's chief end is to glorify God, and to enjoy Him forever." But this verse declares that God plans and works "for *our* [that is, human] glorification."

To glorify anyone or anything is to openly manifest the hidden values within. God glorifies Himself when He reveals Himself to us. John says of Jesus, "The Word was made flesh . . . and we beheld His glory." What was that glory? John tells us precisely, ". . . full of grace and truth" (John 1:14). That was the glory of Jesus: grace and truth!

What, then, is the glory of man? It is to display outwardly all that God made us to be! It is to be a whole person! The truly fascinating thing is that this is what every person, without exception, wants to be! Listen to people talking and you will hear it expressed everywhere. "I want to be me!" "I'm looking for fulfillment." "I'm trying to get my act together."

What we are sent to preach is clearly what everyone everywhere desperately wants to find!

But this is the tragedy of much modern preaching. Preachers have come to believe that the average person no longer has any religious interest and so they appeal to knowledge or science or philosophy. If this lack of religious interest appears to be true, it is because preaching has failed to clarify that what men eagerly want to find—the secret of human fulfillment—is what God lovingly offers to give! True preaching, the preaching of the secret and hidden wisdom of God, will result in human glorification, the actual fulfillment of our deepest desires.

This hidden wisdom, as Paul declares plainly, is "Jesus Christ and Him crucified" (1 Cor. 2:2). It is a message so totally different from the thinking of the world that it constitutes an offense! It declares that until we are changed by a gracious act of God, our highest efforts and most clever schemes for self-improvement will not only prove ineffective—they will actually make things worse! By trying to control our own destiny and run our own world, we will end by not only destroying ourselves but our world as well. Do we need anything else but history or the newspaper to confirm that?

On a recent visit to Stanford University, Malcolm Muggeridge summed up the approaching end of western civilization in this remarkable quote from an American critic, Leslie Fiedler:

> The final conclusion would seem to be whereas other civilizations have been brought down by attacks of barbarians from without, ours had the unique distinction of training its own destroyers at its own educational institutions and providing them with facilities for propagating their destructive ideology far and wide all at the public expense.
>
> Thus did Western man decide to abolish himself, creating his own boredom out of his own affluence, his own vulnerability out of his own strength, his own impotence out of his own erotomania, himself blowing the trumpet that brought the walls of his own city tumbling down. And, having convinced himself that he is too numerous, labors with pill and scalpel and syringe to make himself fewer, until at last, having educated himself into imbecility and polluted and drugged himself into stupefaction, he keels over, a weary, battered old brontosaurus, and becomes extinct.[2]

Though brilliantly stated, this is scarcely hyperbole. It is happening all around us and is an inescapable result of human wisdom.

65

The Wisdom of God Exposes the Incredible Blunders
Which Human Wisdom Makes

"None of the rulers of this age understood this; for if they had, they would not have crucified the Lord of Glory" (1 Cor. 2:8). Here were keen, intelligent men, priding themselves on their ability to govern, to make decisions, and to understand humanity. Yet when Truth Himself appeared before them they could not recognize Him. They totally misunderstood and mishandled Him, and then they nailed Him to a cross. That tendency to commit terrible blunders is characteristic of the wisdom of the world. It is the reason why we live on a polluted planet today torn by strife and schism, and threatened by violence and meaninglessness on all sides. It is the business of preaching to identify such blunders and to help those who fail to see these errors in society today.

Listen to any television news broadcast and in the course of it you will be exposed to fifteen or twenty commercials urging you to buy a product, take a trip, or spend your money in some other way. Note how many times you hear the word "deserve." "You deserve this—you've got it coming to you—you're the kind of person who has a right to expect this." "You deserve a break today!" Gradually listeners begin to believe this subtle propaganda until they lose all sense of gratitude. We do not feel grateful when we finally get what we feel we have long deserved—we are only angry that we did not get it sooner or that we did not get as much as someone else. And if we do not get it at all, we feel resentful and abused.

The media is unknowingly producing a nation of angry, resentful people who are dissatisfied with all they have. And since gratitude is the chief ingredient of joy, we find ourselves in the midst of a people who seek fun continually but are unable to know true joy. And this includes thousands of Christians! It is the business of the preacher to point out these effects and direct people to the true source of joy. The truth is, we do not deserve any good thing! We belong to a race that deserves to be eliminated from the earth. Because we live in continual enmity against God, and in rebellion to His laws, we deserve death. But that is not what we are given! By the grace and mercy of a loving God, we are given life—often long lives—and we are given beauty, family love, food and shelter, and many other blessings. Even more, we are given opportunities to learn the truth and receive forgiveness, acceptance, love, peace—and joy!

Because of these undeserved gifts, our normal attitude should be gratitude. This is why Scripture exhorts us continually to give thanks. Every good and perfect gift comes, as James tells us, "from above . . . from the Father of lights, with whom there is no variation or shadow of turning" (James 1:17). Even those gifts we call trials are from the same source, sent to make us do what we do not want to do, in order to be what we have always wanted to be!

When Paul began to preach this message in Corinth, in dependence on the power of the Spirit, Corinth began to change. Acts 18:8 says, "Many of the Corinthians, hearing, believed and were baptized." There sprang up in that pagan city a group of changed people. They lost their fears and their despair. Under the impact of new life from within, they were gradually changed into loving, caring, wholesome people. Some still struggled with the residues of their past, but the city was never the same again. And as a result, the history of the world changed as well.

There is much more I could say, but perhaps this is enough to help us see the enormous consequences of true preaching and the terrible blight that falls upon a congregation or community which is deprived of these unsearchable riches of Christ. My plea is, let preachers stop feeding people with moral platitudes and psychological pablum. Let us say once more, with Jeremiah, "Your words were found, and I ate them, and Your Word was to me the joy and rejoicing of my heart" (Jer. 15:16).

NOTES

1. John H. Stek, "Interrogating the Bible," *Christianity Today* 30 (14): pp. 21–22.
2. Quoted in Duncan Williams, *Trousered Apes* (New Rochelle, N.Y.: Arlington House, 1972).

Scripture quotations in this article are from the NEW KING JAMES VERSION of the Bible. Copyright © 1979, 1980, 1982 by Thomas Nelson, Inc., Publishers.

Hooting Owls on Tombstones

D. STUART BRISCOE

An old Texas preacher once told me that when he stood before his congregation to preach they looked to him like hooting owls sitting on tombstones. I had no difficulty imagining those poor people sitting in their pews, motionless, impassively looking at him with wide, uncomprehending eyes. I wondered how he could steel himself to face them week after week. On reflection, however, it occurred to me that there was probably some connection between their attitude and his preaching and perhaps I should be wondering how they managed to steel themselves to listen to him week after week! Perhaps they were uncomprehending because he was incomprehensible. Could it be that they were unmoved because they could not see any relevance in what he had to say?

An English vicar with his mind on decaying buildings announced one day that the offertory about to be taken would be devoted in its entirety to the extermination of dry rot in the pulpit and worms in the pew. Inadvertently he had touched a nerve. Not infrequently the rot in the pulpit is so dry that it causes the people to wriggle wearily through dark, subterranean passages of thought without any real sense of direction or hope of arrival. Whether the problem be worms in pews or owls on tombstones, we need to ask, "How is it possible for a message as electrifying as the Christian gospel to be presented in such a way that it is greeted with something less than euphoria and responded to with something less than enthusiasm?" There are, no doubt, many answers to the question, ranging from the spiritual hardness of the hearers to the technical ineptitude of the preacher. But for our purposes we will concentrate on an essentially practical consideration—the matter of relevance in preaching.

I am often reminded that we do not have to make the Scriptures relevant—they are relevant. That is, no doubt, true. But that does not mean that the people in the pews, or more importantly, the ones who never make it as far as the pews, know it. They need to be shown the connection between the pronouncements of the pulpit and the concerns of the people.

Ezra and his contemporaries knew what it meant to communicate effectively with the people. Their approach was as simple as it was effective. Standing before the people on "a high wooden platform built for the occasion . . . they read from the Book of the Law of God, making it clear and giving the meaning so that the people could understand what was being read" (Neh. 8:4, 8). The effectiveness of the preaching was clearly demonstrated by the way the people warmly embraced the message. They gave it their full attention, it changed their attitudes, and they promptly took appropriate action. What more could a preacher wish for, and what more could a congregation desire! We cannot, of course, minimize Ezra's special preparation for the task. He "had devoted himself to the study and observances of the Law of the Lord and to teaching its decrees and laws in Israel" (Ezra 7:10). Neither can we overlook the source and the content of his message. He was committed to "the Book" (Neh. 8). Let us see how Ezra and his friends proclaimed the message of God's Word.

Proclamation

Atmosphere

One of the most remarkable things about Ezra's preaching was that, apparently, the people demanded it. His contemporaries did not have to be dragged to church; rather, "they assembled as one man . . . (and) . . . they told Ezra, the scribe, to bring the Book" (Neh. 8:1). A climate had been created in which people were eager to gather and to hear. Contemporary preachers need to give careful attention to producing the kind of atmosphere to which people are attracted. They need to heed the words of Charles H. Spurgeon, who said, "Pleasantly profitable let all our sermons be."[1]

Attention

There are two things about attention that demand our attention! The first is how to get it and the second is how to keep it. Ezra managed to minister from "daybreak till noon . . . and all the people listened attentively" (Neh. 8:3). He must have been doing something right. Nowadays they tell me that if I have not struck oil in twenty minutes, I should stop boring!

69

The choice of subject matter is clearly of prime importance and depends on who we are trying to reach. Every church has its faithful remnant who will be there on Sunday morning whatever the preacher has to say, but the people who inhabit the periphery, from which growth comes, are not so willing to surrender their allegiance and hand over their attention. Their attention must be earned—or grabbed! But how?

Ezra maintained a critical balance in his message. It was God-centered but people-related. Today there is great discussion about felt needs, and rightly so. But we must not forget that behind every felt need lurks a real need. To address the real need while ignoring the felt need is to guarantee the people will stay away in droves. To deal with the felt need at the expense of the real need is to affirm that they might just as well have stayed at home! The real need of all people is a proper relationship with God; the feltness of this need shows up in innumerable shapes and forms. The preacher who gets and keeps people's attention does it by addressing felt needs in such a way that the people can be led uncomplaining to an understanding of real need.

Some time ago a lady approached me after a service and said, "When are you going to say something relevant?" I asked her what she would like me to talk about and she said, "Life in the family."

I had just finished a series on the fruit of the Spirit, so I said, "Is there a lack of love at home?" "Yes," she responded. "Is there not much joy?" "Absolutely," she replied. "Is there more war than peace?" . . . and so on. Her felt needs were for answers to her family problems. Her real needs were spiritual and needed the ministry of the Holy Spirit—my recent sermon topic—but she had not made the connection. I had apparently not helped much either!

If subject matter is important, so also is pulpit manner. Martyn Lloyd-Jones asserted that "a dull preacher is a contradiction in terms," adding that on one occasion he witnessed a preacher "talking about fire as if he was sitting on an iceberg."[2] The preacher must know the subject so thoroughly that he believes it with intensity and feels it with abandon. Gripped by his message, he becomes transported by it. Living in it, he becomes captivated by it, resulting in an unconscious surrendering of himself—mind, spirit, emotions, and body—to the compelling force of the truth he proclaims. The pulpit is no place for iceberg squatters!

Action

When Ezra preached, the amount of action would have pleased Demosthenes, who reputedly said the three most important things in oratory were action, action, and action. "All the people could see [Ezra] because he was standing above them; and as he opened [the Book] the people all stood up. Ezra praised the LORD, the great God; and all the people lifted their hands and responded, 'Amen! Amen!' Then they bowed down and worshiped the LORD with their faces to the ground" (Neh. 8:5, 6). There was a lot of standing and arm raising and bowing going on when Ezra spoke, and while tastes differ in this regard in the contemporary church, there is little doubt in my mind that the more active and demonstrative the preacher, the more involved and intrigued the people. Nothing is more likely to lull people to sleep than a droning talk emanating from an expressionless face belonging to someone anchored behind a desk. On the other hand, nothing is more likely to carry along a contemporary, visually-oriented people than a messenger whose body has become a medium of communication. One particularly expressive and active preacher had so captivated the attention and interest of one of the young members of his congregation that the child asked his mother with some degree of consternation, "What happens if that man gets out of his box?" Sad to say, the thought never occurs to many people, young or old, apparently because the preacher in question appears to be perfectly content to stay in his pulpit and they are happy to keep him there!

Authority

Modern people are notoriously skittish about authority. This poses a problem for preachers, whose mission is to get people to submit to divine principles and to believe divine promises. Ezra's ministry was so convincing that the people were more than prepared to accept the word from the LORD through him, even when it meant implementing the most far-reaching changes in their lives. How to achieve this today is something which the modern preacher must address. But it is clear to me that if people have not been gripped by the message and messenger, they will not see the need to radically alter their values and lifestyles. A powerfully and winsomely relevant message and a messenger whose words ring of truth and integrity, can bring about change and transformation. Otherwise, preaching has about as much impact as rain on a hot tin roof.

71

Explanation

Explanation Requires Clarification

Making it clear and giving the meaning were priorities in Ezra's preaching. This surely is the real meaning of the word *exposition*. Charles H. Spurgeon explained it neatly when he said, "Having nothing to conceal we have no ambition to be obscure"[3] and Ian MacPherson quoted Dr. James Denney as saying, "The man who shoots above the target does not thereby prove that he has superior ammunition. He simply proves that he is not an accurate shot."[4] If the target is the mind, emotion, and will of the people, the preacher's task is to enter the thought patterns of the congregation so that he will bridge that most awesome of chasms—the gap between what was said and what was heard. If the preacher speaks warmly of grace, he will achieve little if his hearer's only acquaintance with Grace is a blue-eyed blond, and it will not help when he links grace with faith if the hearer's vision of Faith is a brown-eyed brunette. Definition should be tirelessly given, and at the same time cliches should be mercilessly avoided. Definition leads from the dark valley of confusion to the heady heights of comprehension. Weeding cliches ensures that the hearer is spared further struggles in resisting the downward pull into the swamps of irrelevance and meaninglessness.

Clarification Demands Illustration

In a recent preaching class for seminary graduates I asked the students what they hoped to gain from the time of study. Unanimously they said, "We need help with illustration and application." I was surprised at first, but upon further reflection I remembered that a seminary can teach theology, doctrine, hermeneutics, and homiletics, but only experience can teach illustration and application.

Illustrations Should Illumine

John Stott reminds us that "the word 'illustrate' means to illumine, to throw light or lustre upon an otherwise dark object."[5] Given the lack of comprehension of the owls on tombstones, one has to wonder if the entrance of some light and lustre might not have given their imagination wings and set their spirits soaring.

Our Lord illustrated difficult truths in familiar terms that were readily grasped. He showed that the work of the Spirit is like the invisible blowing of the wind, and that the spontaneous expansion of the kingdom is like yeast in dough. His methodology of arguing from the known to the unknown, the concrete to the abstract, and the easily grasped to the hard to understand is plain to see and easy to emulate with a little effort.

Illustrations also Serve to Stimulate Interest

They ring a bell, switch on a light, strike a chord. A preacher who is in touch with his audience must be able to sense when his material is too heavy or his meaning is unclear. If he realizes this during preparation, he can take time to find a good illustration, but if he discovers it during the sermon, he will have to dig deep in his store of helpful anecdotes while thinking on his feet. I am not encouraging this practice, but I have found it to be very helpful on occasion. Many a congregation has breathed a sigh of relief when they have seen a story on the horizon. Stories provide welcome relief from arduous thinking. Like a seventh inning stretch, they relieve the tired muscles of the mind and set the sinews of the spirit in place for what is yet to come.

Illustrations Should Be Intriguing

They should capture the imagination and help the listener retain the message in the recall chamber of the mind. Many preachers comment sadly that often their congregations seem to remember only the illustrations. This may be true. But the remembered illustration may help the mind recall the truth later on through the work of the Spirit. Better to remember the illustration than remember nothing at all!

Illustrations Should Be Inviting

A well-placed illustration will establish rapport. A friend told me that his young son was sitting reluctantly in church one Sunday when I mentioned the name of a local ballplayer who was hitting home runs at a torrid rate. At the mention of the well known name, the boy shot up in his seat, listened intently to what I said, stayed with me through the application, and talked enthusiastically about it on the way home!

A well-placed illustration should also promote empathy. A personal anecdote which clarifies a theological principle is invaluable and, if the hearer can sense the speaker's sincerity, a bridge has been built over which the flow of truth can proceed unhindered. I saw this happen re- 73 cently. My wife illustrated a point by talking about the struggle she went through years ago with one of our teenage children. The women appreciated the fact that the speaker not only knew the subject but had experienced the pain herself and had discovered resources which could help them too.

Illustrations Involve Perspiration

W. E. Sangster wrote, "The craft of sermon illustrations . . . is fun. It is an occupation of leisure. It rests a mind tired of grappling with heavier things. It is a recreation with which to reward yourself at the end of a weary day."[6] Now should my reader find the search for sermon illustration such a delight, I will by no means disagree. In fact, I would testify in some measure to its being true in my experience. But I have to add that it also takes discipline and hard work to incorporate illustrations in preaching. Oftentimes I have become so absorbed in working out the truth in a passage that, like a builder totally absorbed with putting up a wall, I have overlooked the need for a window!

The Work of Sermon Illustration Involves Digging Them Out

I am often asked, "What is the most useful source of illustrations?" That is a difficult question because so much depends on the people who are being addressed. Bearing in mind that an illustration is usually taken from something with which people are familiar, it is obvious that the hearers will, to a large extent, determine the source of an illustration. If the listeners are biblically oriented, then the Bible itself is a wonderful source. For example, when Paul talked of being compelled to preach, (1 Cor. 9:16) he used the same word Matthew used to describe the way Jesus "made the disciples get into the boat" (Matt. 14:22) when apparently they sensed that a storm was brewing. A description of Jesus' making the reluctant disciples get on board can serve to show some of Paul's motivation for preaching. On the other hand, if you are talking to a group of men you cannot go wrong with sports stories or business analogies. In the same way, women always enjoy stories about children, and children are always ready for a laugh. The key is to keep your eyes and ears open for incidents, quotes, and stories which ring a bell in your mind and suggest that they will get a point across.

Fitting Them In

The preacher should always be sensitive to the learning capacity of the listeners. When dealing with abstract concepts, concrete examples are vital. I often tell people, "That is the abstract concept, now let me pour concrete on it!" A good rule of thumb is never to proclaim an abstract concept without marrying it to a concrete example. In the same way, the preacher should be aware that his hearers, after a certain amount of time, will be ready for a little light and luster to alleviate the heaviness of a solemn message. They may not say it out loud, but their body language will often tell the preacher, "Give me a break!" The wise preacher will provide it for them.

Getting Them Across

Recently while preaching through Romans I came to the passage in the eleventh chapter relating to the breaking off of the olive branches, Israel, and the grafting in of wild olive branches, the Gentiles. I wondered if I should explain how grafting works but decided against it. I doubted if even a few people in the congregation had ever done it, and I suspected even fewer would be remotely interested. So instead I told the story of the early days of my only pastorate when the church had an influx of wild kids from the counterculture of the sixties. I told of the struggles in getting the old stalwarts to accept them. There was an amazing reaction both from former "wild branches" and from those who had constituted the resistant old stock. The former, many in tears, expressed great gratitude for what God had done; the latter spoke quietly of the lessons in acceptance they had been forced to learn. All came away with a deeper sense of the grace and mercy of God because they saw afresh His concern for Israel, His adaptability through Israel's rejection of Jesus, and His commitment to relentlessly working out His purposes for both Jews and Gentiles. The message made sense on the grand scale because so many of the people had experienced a similar situation on a personal scale. Accordingly, they lived afresh in a broader understanding of the sovereign Lord.

Making Them Stick

A young man once told me that he remembered hearing me preach some twenty years earlier when he had been a small boy. He even remembered the title of my sermon! Naturally, I was surprised and delighted and

75

could not resist asking him what it was. "Six things we must never forget," he replied with great emphasis, then added to my chagrin, "but I'm afraid I can't remember what they were!" I suppose it was asking too much to expect him to remember what he was not supposed to forget, particularly as many of us have to admit that our memories are things we use to forget with! However there is something to be said for endeavoring to make important points stick in people's memories.

As a teenage schoolboy I heard Dr. Paul Rees preach about Paul's wanting to go on living while at the same time being eager to meet the Lord. What made his exposition stick in my mind was the way he talked about Shakespeare's famous line, "To be, or not to be, that is the question." He explained how the Prince of Denmark wanted to die because life was so awful, but shrank from taking his life because death was even more awful. Dr. Rees then took Shakespeare's famous words, applied them to Paul, and had Paul saying "To be or not to be, that is the question! If I go on living it will be wonderful because Christ is my life, but if I die, so be it because death is my gain." I think the illustration stuck because suddenly a difficult concept made sense. It captured my imagination because I was becoming fascinated with Shakespeare and because, with an ingenious touch, it contrasted the hopelessness of the one man with the hope-filled outlook of the other. It used a pithy, memorable, familiar expression to nail down what a Christian's attitude to life and death should be. Obviously, I have not forgotten the illustration! To this day I never think of Paul's dilemma in any other terms than "To be or not to be!"

Application

The result of Ezra's preaching was that the people were overcome with emotion. They wept and mourned to such an extent that the Levites had to calm them saying, "Be still, for this is a sacred day. Do not grieve" (Neh. 8:11). The people needed specific instructions: "Go and enjoy choice food and sweet drinks, and send some to those who have nothing prepared" (Neh. 8:10). This was the best kind of application. It was direct, clear, and specific. There comes a time in every sermon when preacher and hearer must confront what I like to call the "so-what hump." Assuming the people have been carried (or swept) along by the preaching, there will come a time when a little voice will be asking, "What exactly is the point of all this and how does this relate to me and what am I supposed to do about it?" In my experience, people need help negotiating the "so-what hump." I must admit that I have often failed to give them the help they need. I often assume that it is perfectly obvious what action people should take in response to the message, but my friends tell me that I should not assume it is as clear to everyone else! There is danger, of course, in spelling the application out in such detail that the response is little more than an unthinking reaction to what is being forcefully laid out. There must be personal assimilation of truth if there is to be a genuine application of the message. Many preachers offer an invitation to elicit response. This is helpful to many people and deeply disconcerting to others. Preachers should look for different ways of application so that all kinds of people may be encouraged to respond freely as the Spirit leads.

Spurgeon, on one occasion, told the people to go home, take a piece of paper, and write on it either the word "FORGIVEN" or the word "CONDEMNED." That is one way of applying things in no uncertain terms. A friend of mine told me recently that over thirty years ago she heard Ian Thomas preach and, as she passed him in the church doorway, he shook her hand, looked her in the eye and said, "Tonight you will sleep either as a forgiven sinner or an unforgiven sinner. Goodnight!" Not surprisingly, she made sure she was a forgiven sinner before turning in for the night!

Implementation

The day after Ezra and his colleagues held their marathon preaching session, the people were back for more! Ezra did not disappoint them. During the study of the Book, the people discovered something that their forefathers had known but had conveniently overlooked: the divine command to celebrate the Feast of Tabernacles. When the people read this instruction and discovered how remiss they and their ancestors had been, they promptly "went out and brought back branches and built themselves booths on their own roofs . . ." (Neh. 8:16). This must have greatly amused and bemused the interested and critical observers, but the people of Jerusalem were not deterred. They set about implementing the word with a will, despite its demanding and costly nature.

A young lady I know was living out of wedlock with a well-known professional athlete in our city at the time she came to faith. In a Bible study shortly after her conversion the word fornication came up. "What's fornication?" she asked in all innocence. The other girls in the group who were her friends answered bluntly, "It's what you and your boyfriend do." She looked bewildered and said, "But it says here that it is wrong" to which the other girls said, "You're dead right, it's wrong." She was quiet for a moment and then said, "Then if it's wrong, it's got to stop and I'm going home to tell him either we get married or I'm leaving." That is implementation!

John Stott asserts that "Preaching is indispensable to Christianity. Who would disagree?"[7] But it is not the preaching that produces owls on tombstones. Rather, it is the kind that makes eagles soar and larks sing.

NOTES

1. Charles H. Spurgeon, "Illustration in Preaching," p. 11.
2. D. Martyn Lloyd-Jones, *Preaching and Preachers* (London: Hodder and Stoughton, 1971), pp. 87, 88.
3. Spurgeon, p. 9.
4. Ian MacPherson, *The Art of Illustrating Sermons* (New York: Abingdon Press, 1964).
5. John R. W. Stott, *Between Two Worlds* (Grand Rapids, Mich.: Eerdmans, 1982), pp. 239, 240.
6. William Edwin Sangster, *The Craft of the Sermon* (London: Epworth Press, 1954), p. 204.
7. Stott, p. 15.

Scripture quotations in this article are from the NEW INTERNATIONAL VERSION of the Bible. Copyright © 1978 by New York International Bible Society.

Interpretation in Preaching

JOEL GREGORY

T hey race to seminars, gather in living rooms, glue their ears to radios, take mail-order courses, collect tapes, glut their bookshelves with multiple volumes, traipse across the country to encampments, and rivet their eyes to blow-dried television preachers. People hunger for a word from God. Even a near-sighted insensitive observer of American religious culture could hardly miss the hunger for a word from God on the part of Christian people. Pulpit committees scour the nation and then complain to the seminaries, "Where are the preachers?" What they mean, as often as not, is, "Where is someone who can relate the Word of God to my life?" Markus Barth has gone so far as to call some contemporary preachers traitors to their task.[1] What is the task of homiletical interpretation of Scripture? In attempting to answer that question in this study, I pay tribute to Stephen F. Olford. Dr. Olford is effectively calling preachers in our day back to the task of anointed expository preaching. It has been my privilege to lecture at the Stephen Olford Center for Biblical Preaching in Memphis, Tennessee, and to witness what Dr. Olford and his staff are doing for preachers who desperately need help in the art of expository preaching.

What is wrong with preaching? Every generation produces a covey of critics.[2] In 1976 Robert Middleton blamed the weakness of preaching on the debasement of language itself, the loss of rational thought in American culture, and the failure to relate preaching to the political needs of the times. He even blames the "musicalization" of American culture which constantly assaults people "in restaurant, elevator, subway; there is no escape."[3] Yet in his entire study there is not a single mention of the loss of the Bible in contemporary preaching.

Nelson Bell more accurately diagnoses the disease by comparing the contemporary sermon to surgery without a knife. In an immaculate and fully supplied operating room, a highly trained team of surgeons prepares the anesthetized patient for surgery. The chief surgeon picks up one instrument after another and makes futile passes over the patient. This goes on for an hour, after which the patient is wheeled out to a recovery room. Before long, it becomes obvious that the patient is getting weaker. Indeed, the surgeon has many such patients showing no signs of recovery. At a general staff meeting to investigate the problem, an unpromising, dull intern dared to say it: "Mr. Chief of Staff," he said, "I have scrubbed in on a number of these unsuccessful operations, and there is one thing I have repeatedly noticed: the surgeon does not use the knife. There is no incision, no bleeding, no going down to the source of the illness. Nothing is removed. When the patient leaves the operating room, he is in exactly the same condition as when he came in."

Bell proceeds to accuse the contemporary sermon of a similar fault. Distinguished men in beautiful facilities never do the very thing that is at the center: get out the Word of God to the people.[4]

Dr. Stephen Olford has sought to help preachers avoid the ridiculous posture of a surgeon without a knife. Central to his concern stands the interpretation of Scripture in preaching. This article addresses those concerns of biblical interpretation as they relate to preaching. This modest effort does not intend to discuss trends in contemporary preaching. That has been done well by others.[5] This study will demonstrate, first of all, the critical importance of biblical context in preaching. Then, the major portion of the article deals with grammatical and syntactical interpretation. Especially significant is emphasis on the necessity of biblical languages for mature interpretation. Finally, the article addresses the necessity for imagination in interpretation. Even for the most conservative, cautious interpreter the distance between the study desk and the pulpit seems to be a great chasm. Getting the word from Palestine to Pittsburgh, from Jerusalem to Jersey, challenges all those who confess that God's Word cannot err. Often between the study desk and the pulpit the text "seems to have passed through a mysterious underground process of filtering, like the Danube River, whose water, it is true, reappears,— but then it is flowing into the Rhine."[6] No one bridge helps the interpreter cross that chasm. He may study the history of preaching and see how others crossed it. He may study homiletical principles codified in a hundred books. He may observe contemporary examples of preaching. Yet having done all that, the central act of preaching may elude him: getting the Word of God out of the then into the now in this Sunday's sermon. One may count on his fingers the number of books that even attempt to bridge this gap between exegesis and pulpit. That is the very act of interpretation for preaching.

Some may assert that the ability to make the Word live in the act of preaching is a gift. Mezger correctly asserts, "This is connected with the conviction that the crucial factor in preaching, just as in art, cannot be taught because it must be 'given' a person; but also with the conviction that a great deal can be taught, and that the position as well as the situation of the sermon can be changed for the better, if the preparation for preaching is properly carried out."[7] Even the most gifted preachers admit they do not always leap that chasm between then and now. Luther himself concluded sermons with the confession that he had only partially come to grips with the text. Praiseworthy was his practice of confessing, "We will hear more of this at another time. May God grant that others after me do better."[8] When have you heard a sermon end with that confession?

Nevertheless, the preacher like Jacob has entered into a lifelong wrestling match with the text. He wrestles with the text to compel it to give him the twofold blessing: what is said then and what it says now. The preacher does this by addressing the literary-contextual, historico-grammatical, and mood-imaging aspects of the text.

Context

Barrett recalls a discussion between his father and a noted Methodist preacher of an earlier day:

"When I have found a text," said my father, "I always begin by studying the context in order to make sure of its original setting and meaning." "When I find a text," replied his companion, "I never look up the context for fear it spoils the sermon." That is dishonest; that is handling the word of God deceitfully.[9]

As Robinson notes, "setting the passage within its wider framework simply gives the Bible the same chance we give the author of a paperback."[10] You would hardly read a single paragraph on page 100 of an Agatha Christie novel. Yet countless preachers drag texts out of their context every Sunday while the text screams, "I don't want to go; please don't make me leave here." Chalmer E. Faw accuses the whole Christian world of having the "dread disease of fragmentosis subjectivosis . . . frag-mentizing the Bible along the lines of their own subjective predilections or theological leanings."[11] This fragmenting tendency may have been unin-tentionally aided by the French printer Robert Estienne (Stephanus), who versified an edition of the Greek Testament in 1551. The Geneva Bible (1560) and the King James Version (1611) followed. The indentation of each verse, however, leaves the erroneous impression that every verse stands on its own without context. While this may be true of John 3:16, it is hardly the case of a single verse in Leviticus, for example.

Jesse James Northcutt, Professor of Preaching Emeritus at Southwest-ern Baptist Theological Seminary, by teaching and example has demon-strated the significance of biblical context for preaching. He defines several levels of context:

> The immediate context consists of those verses or paragraphs immediately preceding or following a passage. The remote context is that portion of Scripture less closely related to the passage and may embrace paragraphs, a chapter, or even an entire book of Scripture. Beyond the remote context there is the larger context of the development of thought in the Bible itself. The principle of progressive revelation calls for a passage being interpreted in the light of its relation to the stages of development of biblical writers.[12]

Northcutt's masterful sermon on Philippians 1:1–12, *A Drama in Christian Joy,* demonstrates throughout the excellent homiletical use of each contextual level mentioned above. The sermon opens with a refer-ence to the book context, emphasizing the recurrence of *joy* throughout the four chapters.[13] Northcutt then moves to the canonical context, relat-ing Philippians to Paul's expressed desire to preach in Rome (Rom. 1:13). He then turns to the historical context of the imperial guards who watched Paul, describing their position in Roman society. Next, he touches the immediate context in Philippians 1:15–16 concerning those jealous of Paul.[14] He returns to the historical context with a description of Nero. He concludes by relating the canonical context, his imprisonment in Rome (Rom. 1:6). The entire message is virtually a reverent meditation on the levels of context of the Philippian letter.[15]

The canonical, remote, and immediate literary context of a passage figures as the first step in the evangelical approach to historico-grammatical interpretation for preaching. The canonical context locates the passage in question in the larger stream of biblical revelation. For example, in preaching from Nehemiah, the interpreter must first ask, "Where does Nehemiah's ministry and message fit into the larger history that began with God's call of Abraham and culminating in the ministry of Jesus?" The fact that Nehemiah lived in Artaxerxes' winter palace at Susa around 444 B.C. locates him in time and space in the unfolding sequence of God's mighty acts. To fail to locate Nehemiah in the post-exilic period of restoration would be fatal to an appropriate understanding of his work. Yet canonical context is more often than not ignored in preaching.

This does not call for yawn-provoking lectures on ancient history. A few apt phrases in the introduction of a biblical sermon can set the canonical context in a memorable way. One might introduce a sermon from Nehemiah with the following contextual remarks:

> Steve Allen hosted a captivating television program on the educational network. Each week he seated around the same table great figures from various centuries and diverse fields. He might host Alexander the Great, Woodrow Wilson, Florence Nightingale, and Joseph Stalin. It would be fascinating to gather around your table the great men who lived during the eighty years of Nehemiah's life and ministry. You would seat the great Greek dramatists Aeschylus and Aristophanes, the noted historians Herodotus and Thucydides, as well as the philosophers Socrates and Plato. Yet sitting with them would be a rugged Jewish layman with a single vision. While they spoke of philosophy and history, Nehemiah would tell how he built the wall that mattered for God.

Without being heavy-handed and with some imagination, the interpreter may present such contextual material in creative ways.

The remote context concerns the location of a passage in the total scheme of a biblical book. The thoughtful expositor should always indicate that context in his message, either in the introduction or within the exposition of the passage. For example, in 1 Peter 4:12 the apostle warns, "Dear friends, do not be surprised at the painful trial you are suffering, as though something strange were happening to you" (NIV). The interpretation of this verse should not ignore the remote context in 1 Peter 1:6 ". . . though now for a little while you may have suffered grief in all kinds of trials." These two passages have a mutual and reciprocal relation in context. You can understand neither one without the other. The first clarifies the breadth and purpose of the trials. The latter underscores the na-

83

ture of the trials, literally "fiery trials" at the hand of local police action and persecution among the recipients. The exposition of either verse would be anemic without recourse to the other in remote context.

The immediate context involves those verses directly attached to the passage being preached. A book such as James presents a particular challenge in determining and communicating immediate context. Some feel that James is no more than a book of detached aphorisms, sapiential literature such as Proverbs with little contextual relationship. Others feel that James does have contextual relationships. James 1:2–8 addresses the multicolored trials of believers, with the admonition that they ask for wisdom in the trials. James 1:9–11 contrasts the humble poor with the arrogant rich. On the surface these two paragraphs appear to have no connection at all. On closer examination, however, James picks up the word "trial" again in 1:12. This should tip off the preacher that 1:9–11 deals with two specific kinds of trials: the trial of affluence and the trial of poverty. Where there appears to be no context, there indeed is a contextual relationship that makes the preaching of 1:9–11 more than random remarks about the rich and poor.

In addition to the literary context discussed above, the historical context also demands attention. Sometimes this research is given the name *isagogics*. That simply means studies which lead into the understanding of a passage. Typical isagogical concerns are the author, recipients, date, occasion, peculiar historical and geographical concerns, and any other related matters in the deeper background of the text. In a recent excellent exegetical manual, Fee suggests the interpreter attempt to discover these matters himself in the preliminary reading of the text.[16] While this should be attempted, the busy pastor will also find these matters fully discussed in standard Old and New Testament introductions as well as in the front matter of any monograph on a biblical book.

Ignoring context produces sermons that would sometimes be humorous if they were not so tragic. Years ago there was an occasion which honored the anniversary of a religious magazine, whose logo was a beacon. At the commemorative banquet there was even a beacon revolving on top of a stand. The theme for the evening honored the journal as "a beacon atop the impregnable rock of Holy Scripture." The message from the motto was grounded in Isaiah 30:17, "One thousand shall flee at the rebuke of one; at the rebuke of five shall ye flee: till ye be left as a beacon upon the top of a mountain, and as an ensign on a hill." Totally ignoring the context in Isaiah 30, the leadership seized on the single phrase, "a beacon upon the top of a mountain." In fact, that phrase in context makes exactly the opposite of the intended assertion. In context, Isaiah warned the inhabitants not to make an alliance with Egypt out of unbelief in God's power to deliver. If Israel made such a pagan alliance, her enemies would so overpower her that Israel would be abandoned on a mountain with no defense in sight. Indeed, she would be as exposed and helplessly visible to her enemies as a beacon on top of a mountain. One supposes that the patrons of the worthy journal did not actually wish to make the point that their magazine was a sitting duck helplessly exposed to even the weakest attacker! Yet that is exactly the point of Isaiah 30:17. Beware of context.

Grammar

Grammatical Elements in Interpretations

Ray Summers writes, "Basic to all competent approaches in New Testament study is the historico-critical method . . . It is the only method which keeps the exegete in continuous dialogue with the text he seeks to understand."[17] The cornerstone of such methodology is the accurate examination of the grammatical constructs of the text.

The exposition of Scripture cannot avoid the exposition of words. As such, the exegete-preacher must deal with the variables presented in the words, phrases, and clauses of Scripture. At the most basic level, words have phonology—a certain sound. The English *amen* transliterates the Aramaic by the same sound. *Hosanna* is a rough translation of the Hebrew *hoshea na,* which means "save now." Phonology seldom plays a large role in interpretation. Morphology means the form of a word. As such it plays a crucial role in interpretation. The declension of nouns and the conjugation of verbs reflect their morphology or form. Verbs vary in mood, voice, tense, person, and number. Nouns vary in case: vocative, nominative, dative, ablative, genitive, objective. Each of these influences the translation and interpretation of a passage.

Lexicology considers the meaning of words. As such it addresses etymology, which studies the roots or primitive meanings of biblical words. In New Testament studies this involves the careful study of classical, hellenic, hellenistic, koine, and patristic Greek. Lexicology does not stop with etymology. It further studies the historical development of a word, its usage in various contexts, and comparative synonyms to distinguish that word from similar words. The responsible preacher must use all of these tools to establish the *usus loquendi,* the meaning of the words at the time of the author.

Three resources for lexicological studies aid the interpreter. The first of these are Bible dictionaries and encyclopedias. These provide general and specific treatments as well as further bibliographic information. Biblical word books and lexicons provide more specific explanation on individual words. These come in both single volumes that deal with more prominent words and multiple-volume sets on both the Old and New Testaments. Although dealing with the original languages, such tools may also help the English Bible student. A third source is biblical concordances. Although these do not give definition of words, they do demonstrate usage in context which may in fact give more definitive understanding than lexicons.[18]

Fee, in a recent concise handbook for exegesis, gives a helpful list of all grammatical concerns for the serious interpreter:

for nouns/pronouns:	case function (e.g., dative of time, subjective genitive); also antecedent of pronoun
for finite verbs:	significance of tense, voice, mood
for infinitives:	type/usage: (e.g., complementary, in direct discourse)
for participles:	type/usage
	attributive: usage (adjective, substantive)
	supplementary: the verb it supplements
	circumstantial: temporal, casual, attendant circumstance
for adjectives:	the word it modifies
for adverbs:	the word it modifies
for conjunctions:	type (coordinate, adversative, time, cause)
for particles:	the nuance it adds to the sentence.[19]

It is beyond the scope of this study to list the staggering number of aids presently available to the student of English or Hebrew/Greek Bible. The explosion of biblical study aids gives to every student the most comprehensive tools in the history of biblical interpretation.[20] More to the point, there exists a current crisis in grammatical studies. A trend in contemporary American theological studies is the neglect or elimination of biblical language studies. This writer contends that such studies are the cornerstone for continuing excellence in biblical preaching.

Biblical Language in Homiletical Interpretation

Four and one-half centuries have passed since Erasmus wrote the Preface to his Greek Testament. In spite of the imperfections related to that work, for three centuries it was the standard for ministerial linguistic study. Erasmus exclaimed,

> These holy pages will summon up the living image of Christ's mind. They will give you Christ Himself, talking, healing, dying, rising—the whole Christ, in a word. They will give Him to you in an intimacy so close that He would be less visible to you if He stood before your eyes.[21]

Jesse Northcutt believes that a background in biblical languages best prepares the exegete for the task of interpretation for preaching. An examination of his sermons demonstrates a thorough grasp of the principles and practice of using the languages to undergird interpretation in the sermon.

For example, in his sermon *The Forks of the Road* (Heb 11:1, 23–27), Northcutt emphasizes strongly Moses' refusal to be known as the son of Pharaoh's daughter. "The word refused indicates that it was a deliberate decision of renunciation."[22] He bases this interpretation, without doubt, on the aorist verb which emphasizes the punctiliar quality of the refusal in this context. This is only a single evidence of many which indicate his reliance on biblical languages to the grammatico-historical hermeneutic.

Earle Ellis decries that attitude toward biblical language which discounts it in the present clamor for immediate relevance. The view which discounts biblical languages as a basis for preaching leaves the student at the mercy of textbooks written on the high-school level. "No minister who has—however long ago—learned Hebrew or Greek can ever be quite as susceptible as before to a simplistic misuse of the Bible." Whether or not he uses the tool, he has been handed it; his attitude toward the text can never be the same as before exposure to biblical languages.[23]

Without some reference to the languages the minister cannot make a reasoned use of modern literature about the text, consult an analytical commentary, do a word study, or discuss a biblical concept such as *inheritance*. Further, he is impeded in the comparison of the multiple transla-

87

tions and paraphrases available today. Interpretation of Scripture without reference to biblical languages "is like making a lemon meringue pie with a purchased pie shell, ready-mix filling, and aerosol topping—one is 'doing cooking' without having to bother learning to cook."[24] Needless to say, such sermonic cooking usually gives a case of homiletical indigestion. In law school understanding a case is based on a prior knowledge of political science and history. Medical school assumes a background of chemistry and biology. You would not wish to consult a physician whose only study involved bedside manner and prescription writing! The listening congregation deserves like attention to the language of the text.

Scholars often resort to metaphorical language to indicate the value of sermon preparation from the languages. No freezing or canning process can substitute for the freshness of a peach taken directly from the tree. Just as a rose begins to lose an indefinable something as soon as it is picked, even so the text loses something when cut from its roots in the language. In the preface to his reference aid Vincent notes:

> Even as nature fills in the space between the foreground and the background of her landscapes with countless details of form and color, light and shadow, so the rich details of the New Testament words, once apprehended, impart a depth of tone and just relation and perspective to the salient masses of doctrine, narrative, and prophecy . . . How often a picture or bit of history is hidden away in a word, of which a translation gives and can give no hint![25]

Robinson uses a felicitous metaphor when he compares the difference between study and preparation in the translation and the languages to the difference between watching black and white or color television. You see the same show, but the difference is one of color and enjoyment.[26] Northcutt contributed the chapter "Interpreting the Text" to the textbook *Steps to the Sermon,* the standard text at many schools. Northcutt insists, "To understand the text the interpreter must know the kind of language with which he deals, the significance of words, and the relation of the words to each other in the passage."[27] He insists that the first step in interpretation must be attention to verbal analysis of the text. "Grammatical relationships within the passage must be clear if the passage is to be understood. Words mean what they mean as they stand in relationship to each other."[28] The interpreter of the Scripture must be an interpreter of words in every nuance and significance. This means more than a gift for pulpit gab. The expositor of Scripture matures through years of careful and repeated treatment of the biblical languages.

The suggestiveness of careful exegesis for preaching should stand beyond need for demonstration. The obvious absence of such exegetical preparation from contemporary preaching suggests the need for some reminders. The preacher working on Romans 12:1-8 finds a sunburst of meaning in the original text. When he confronts the exhortation, "Be not conformed: but be transformed," he uncovers a dimension of understanding which transforms his sermonic interpretation with the slightest attention to the languages. *Conformed* renders *sunschematizo* and *transformed* renders *metamorphoomai*. The exegete will discover that the former implies "to assume an outward expression that does not come from one's inner being and is not representative of it but is put on from the outside." The present imperative preceded by the negative *me* forbids the continuation of an act already in progress. He might translate, "Stop assuming an outward expression which does not come from within you and is not representative of you but is put on from without and is patterned after this age." A wealth of ideas leaps from this suggestive word. Christians may masquerade as materialists in an outward conformity to current values, while contradicting the inwardness of their spiritual lives.

When the interpreter turns to *metamorphoomai* he discovers a like mother lode of meaning. The simple verb implies "to give outward expression of one's inner being, that expression coming from the being truly representative of the inner being." Sermonic ideas almost assault the exegete from this interpretation. The Christian life reflects an outward expression of an inner nature. Being always precedes doing. For a Christian, to be is to do. What is more, such attention to exegetical detail readily suggests illustrations. Who could not see in the chameleon's ability to change color with the situation a perfect illustration of the two verbs above?[29]

It is especially in tenses that Greek cannot be matched in modern languages. One discovers a sermon in tenses in Romans 6:13. The Authorized Version renders, "Neither present your members unto sin, but present yourself unto God." The first instance of "present" is the simple present which denotes successive, repeated, continuous acts of sin—a way of life and a direction of habitual living. The second "present" pinpoints the aorist imperative, a supreme act of self-surrender which carries with it all future decisions.[30] Again, the exegesis suggests the illustration. When Hernando Cortez arrived at Vera Cruz with six hundred soldiers, he burned his boats in the harbor before marching to the Aztec capital. That decision carried all else with it. It was indeed an aoristic act! One will find that illustrations grow from the native soil of the text and are truly illustrations, not impositions. The writer attests without question that the best illustrations in his sermons always come from suggestions embedded in the exegesis of the text.

An entire outline may take shape from the analysis of a few words of the original text. Consider 1 John 2:1, "We are having an advocate face to face with the Father, Jesus Christ the Righteous One" (author's translation). The noun *parakleton* (advocate, counselor for the defense) repays any study in a theological dictionary. The present tense of the verb *echomen* proclaims that there is never a time when the believer does not have the advocacy of Christ. The preposition *pros* denotes the position of Christ in intimate, face-to-face relationship with the Father. The proper name *Iesous,* from the Hebrew for Joshua, distinguishes the human name of the man from Nazareth. Yet the word Christ with its ordinary usage in Johannine literature identifies that man of Nazareth as none other than the anointed Messiah, Son of God. As such he is *dikaios,* righteous in every respect before God.

From this emerges an exegetical outline determined and contoured by nothing but the text:

    I. Every believer has an advocate
   II. Every believer has an advocate at all times *(echomen)*
  III. Every believer has an advocate in the best place *(pros)*
  IV. Every believer has an advocate of real help
      A. A Sympathetic Advocate—Jesus
      B. An Effective Advocate—Christ
      C. A Righteous Advocate—the Righteous One

If the interpreter only adds fresh, crisp illustration and narrow, specific application, he may stand with confidence that every movement in the sermon finds direct biblical authority.

A single Greek finite verb may determine the outline and explanatory content of an entire sermon. Criswell, in his sermon *The Command to Be Filled with the Spirit,* bases the entire sermon on the mode, tense, number, and voice of the verb in the famous command *plerousthe en penu-*

mati, "be filled with the Spirit" (Eph. 5:18). He begins with an etymological study of several Greek verbal synonyms to distinguish the significance of *pleroo*. Having done that, he develops the body of the message entirely from the morphology of the verb.

I. God commands that we be filled with the Spirit
   Plerousthe is in the imperative mood
II. The filling a repeated experience
   A. *Plerousthe* is in the present tense (which in Greek indicates kind of action—continuous)
   B. *Plerousthe* is plural in number—to every Christian
III. The man under the influence of the Spirit
   Plerousthe is in the passive voice—the believer is acted upon

Here the entire sermon is dictated by the grammatical elements of a single Greek verb. Although not every message could or should be so tied to grammar, in this instance it provides masterful use of grammar in the treatment of a difficult and sensitive object.[31]

To present the findings of lexical, grammatical, and syntactical study, one does not have to sound like Browning's grammarian—dead from the waist down. Studious preachers must always avoid the temptation to take the tools of the trade to the pulpit. Your congregation has a distinct lack of interest in the finer points of the pluperfect middle passive!

When you visit the doctor, you do not expect him to bring out a cadaver and read over it some incomprehensible medical tome. You want him to tell you in plain language why you hurt and how you can get well. Likewise, the congregation expects you to deal with the details of the text, but they wish to hear it in the vernacular. Exegetes should never forget that koine Greek reflects the marketplace and the street corner, not the academy and the stoa of academic remoteness.

Among others, Ward demonstrates an engaging way to present the nuance of Greek verb tenses without the baggage of grammatical jargon. Consider his description of the difference between the aorist and the imperfect tenses.

We have the contrast between pinpoints and panoramas, between shooting Niagara and navigating the rapids. The aorist savours of the staccato, of the brisk striking of a note on the piano, whereas the imperfect holds down the keys of the organ. The aorist drops the curtain; the imperfect shows the players acting on the stage. The aorist corresponds to the 91 short squirt from a boy's water pistol whereas the imperfect is illustrated by the continuous flow of a waterfall.[32]

Few congregations would object to the use of exegetical insight if presented with such lyrical and pictorial quality.

The working pastor, stretched on the rack between returning telephone calls and running to the hospital, may immediately cry foul. Who can administrate the staff and also pour over grammars? Additionally, the pressured pastor responds, "There are so many good translations now. Why should I bother with textual analysis when so many more competent than I have already done the work?" This sounds good, but in reality argues for just the opposite. Since so many translators have become interpreters-in-paraphrase, as never before the pastor needs a basis for comparison. Some learned the languages as if their lifetime occupation would be to teach classics or semitics.

The busy pastor should not hesitate to use any crib necessary to get at the languages in a way he can use them. An interlinear, analytical lexicon, or any other of the many popularizing aids should be used without guilt or apology. In this regard the dictum is "halitosis is better than no breath at all." As Adams observes:

> With all that a busy pastor must do, it is only right for him to employ every available aid that he can afford, to keep his hand into the continued use of Hebrew and Greek. He would be a poor steward of time and energy if he did not. Many men have lost any language ability they once had because they believed . . . that it was wrong to use anything but the naked text and the standard grammars and lexicons.[33]

Syntactical Analysis for Homiletical Structure

More recently a new emphasis in interpretation for the pulpit has emerged. This emphasis promises to make the biblical sermon not only biblical in content but also biblical in shape. The emphasis in question is that of syntactical analysis. The Greek preposition *sun* means "with" and the finite verb *tassein* indicates "to put" or "to place." Thus syntactical analysis emphasizes how words, phrases, and clauses are placed with each other in shaping the biblical narrative. In other words, such analysis indicates in the flow of thought what the biblical writer considered dominant and what he considered subordinate.

Kaiser calls the tool for discovering the structure of narrative a block diagram or syntactical display. Fee favors the more exotic title "sentence flow schematic."[34] By whichever name, the purpose is the same. These procedures yield a visual display of the dominant and subordinate thoughts of the writer. This enables the preacher to shape his outline by the contours of the biblical text.

Childs complained, "Much of the frustration which the preacher experiences in using commentaries stems from the failure of the interpreter to deal with the text in its canonical shape."[35] The analytical, grammatical study of a passage fragments and atomizes the passage. The preacher must have a tool to put the passage back together. At the same time this tool should enable the preacher to move from the "then" of the text to the "now." Syntactical exegesis helps in both regards.

If homiletical sins may be divided into venial and mortal, surely the outrages perpetrated in some sermon outlines border on the mortal. Does not the outline have a right to be shaped by the text as much as the content of the message? To be truly biblical one must contour the message around the contour of the text. Baumann reports an awful abuse of this principle from a sermon on the prodigal son:

I. His Madness
   A. He wanted his tin
   B. He surrendered to sin
   C. He gave up his kin
II. His Badness
   A. He went to the dogs
   B. He ate with the hogs
   C. He hocked all his togs
III. His Gladness
   A. He was given the seal
   B. He ate up the veal
   C. He danced a reel[36]

The syntactical display provides a way out of this forced, artificial outline that often characterizes expository preaching. Consider the following block diagram of 1 Peter 1:3–5 as an approach to shaping a biblical sermon:

Blessed be the God and Father
of our Lord Jesus Christ

93

<pre>
who begat us again
    according to his great mercy
    unto a living hope
    by the resurrection of Jesus Christ from the dead
    unto an inheritance
        incorruptible
        undefiled
        unfading
        kept
            in heaven
            for you
                who are guarded
                    through faith
                    unto salvation
                        ready
                        to be revealed
                            in the last time
</pre>

Note that the more dominant elements in the text tend to the left and the more subordinate elements tend to the right. The central idea of the text may quickly be discovered from the first three lines of the diagram: praise to God for the new birth. Immediately thereafter are four adverbial elements which qualify the new birth. One may readily discover a sermon structure based on the shape of the text itself. By generalizing the adverbial clauses into present, active, transitive statements, the preacher may move the text into the present. Consider the following sermon outline under the title *Birthmarks of the New Birth*:

BIRTHMARKS OF THE NEW BIRTH
1 Peter 1:3–5

Thesis: God marks every believer with identifying marks of the new birth.
    I. The new birth marks you as the recipient of great mercy.
    II. The new birth marks you with living hope.
    III. The new birth marks you with a secure inheritance.

This simple outline demonstrates clearly how syntactical diagrams enable the preacher to discover the shape of the text and structure the outline of the sermon to fit that shape. For example, under III the preacher might wish to pick up the four strong adjectival elements which describe the "secure inheritance." In speaking of the "incorruptible, undefiled, un-fading, kept" inheritance, the expositor can give each adjective the play it deserves in the exposition without majoring on minors or skewing the entire outline to emphasize his favorite theme.

Imagination in Homiletical Exposition

The same sudden Sunday surprise has confronted every prepared preacher. Throughout the week he has labored over text, illustrations, and application. The sermon employs accurate exegesis, unimpeachable her-meneutic and homiletic balance. Yet on Sunday morning it weakly oozes over the pulpit and hardly gets past the Lord's Supper table. One carried the homiletical football to the opponent's ten-yard line, but failed to score a preaching touchdown!

What is missing? Often such fainting fits in the pulpit can be traced to no imagination in the presentation. Although every iota subscript of the text has been studied and the preacher has prayed for the anointing of God, no imagination has been used in the presentation. Jesse Northcutt's sermon from Philippians 1 demonstrates the difference that imagination can make in preaching a well-known passage. Equally spaced throughout the sermon are passages demonstrating imagination in exposition. He uses the leitmotif of the cloudy day broken by the sun:

> When the curtain rises on scene one, it is a dismal, dreary Monday morning in the city of Rome. The setting is the closely confining four walls of Paul's rented house in Rome. With him is a silent, surly Roman soldier. It is one of those days when one awakens with a sense of depression and finds it easier to count his troubles than to count his blessings. Let's suppose that the apostle experienced such a day.[37]

Complimenting the exegesis in the midst of the sermon, Northcutt imagines:

> Even as he began to think of God's goodness, the sun began to break through the clouds and to shine through his small window, piercing the gloom and driving away the chill. There was growing light and warmth where once there was darkness and gloom.[38]

95

Finally, toward the last movement of the sermon he once again uses the motif:

> The sun which had filtered through the small window and had begun to drive away the gloom and chill of Paul's prison was now shining in warmth and brilliance. Possible depression fled before its brilliance.[39]

The violin virtuoso Fritz Kreisler had a flawed technique, but he was nevertheless a great violinist. His greatness came in the imagination with which he interpreted the music. The same may be true of preaching. Few combine Northcutt's exegetical and theological skills with his bright imagination. Yet every interpreter may brighten passages with creative imagery that rests within the legitimate bounds of the text. Although this cannot be taught, Garrison suggests some steps toward it in the intriguingly titled chapter "Think Yourself Out of Your Own Skin":

1. Strive for the viewpoint of a child.
2. Seek the outlook of the novice.
3. Adopt the viewpoint of one who offends.
4. See from the perspective of various backgrounds.
5. Explore the non-human world.
6. Fashion metaphors and epigrams.
7. Extend your sensory experiences.
8. Go outside the familiar.[40]

He concludes with this exhortation: "Thirty seconds from every safe and familiar route, there is a strange world that includes good reasons for the heart to pound. To the degree that you deviate from the sheltered and familiar, you are likely to discover close at hand a new universe of experience."[41]

Surely this generation waits for the pulpiteers who can bring the Middle East of the first century to the Southwest of the 20th century. Some now do and some now unknown certainly will. But those who do will approach the text with a reverent grammatico-historical hermeneutic, an eye to the shape of that text, and with the luminous quality of imagination that will cause yet another generation to say with those who heard that exposition by the Lord who gave the word, "Did not our heart burn within us, while he talked with us by the way, and while he opened to us the scriptures?" (Luke 24:32 KJV).

NOTES

1. Markus Barth, "Biblical Preaching Today," *Review and Expositor* 72 (Spring 1975): 165.

2. Clyde E. Fant, *Preaching for Today* (New York: Harper & Row, 1975), pp. 1–10. He chronicles an amazing variety of criticisms of preaching, especially those during the so-called "Golden Age" of preaching.

3. Robert G. Middleton, "What Is the Matter With Preaching?" *Religion in Life* 45 (Autumn 1976): 299.

4. Nelson Bell, "Missing One Knife," *Christianity Today* 21 (August 1970): 34–35.

5. Harold T. Bryson, "Distinctive Trends in Contemporary Preaching," *The Theological Educator* (Spring 1975): 119–35.

6. Manfred Mezger, "Preparation for Preaching—The Route from Exegesis to Proclamation," trans. Robert A. Kraft, in *Translating Theology into the Modern Age* (New York: Harper & Row, 1965), p. 160. This represents one of a few efforts to move from the study to the pulpit. Particularly helpful are the remarks about translating exegesis into pulpit exposition.

7. Ibid., p. 162.

8. Ibid., p. 168.

9. C. K. Barrett, *Biblical Problems and Biblical Preaching* (Philadelphia: Fortress Press, 1964), p. 37.

10. Haddon W. Robinson, *Biblical Preaching* (Grand Rapids, Mich.: Baker Book House, 1980), p. 58.

11. Chalmer E. Faw, *A Guide to Biblical Preaching* (Nashville: Broadman Press, 1962), p. 58.

12. H. C. Brown, Jr., H. Gordon Clinard, and Jesse Northcutt, *Steps to the Sermon* (Nashville: Broadman Press, 1963), p. 55.

13. Jesse Northcutt, "A Drama in Christian Joy," in *Southwestern Sermons,* ed. H. C. Brown, Jr. (Nashville: Broadman Press, 1960), p. 161.

14. Ibid., p. 162.

15. Ibid., p. 165.

16. Gordon D. Fee, *New Testament Exegesis: A Handbook for Students and Pastors* (Philadelphia: The Westminster Press, 1983), p. 34. This volume provides an exceptionally clear step-by-step procedure for the exegesis of the text. He provides both a long form and a shorter approach for the busy pastor. The table of contents enables the reader to turn immediately to any question he might face in treating the text.

17. Ray Summers, "Contemporary Approaches in New Testament Study," in *The Broadman Bible Commentary,* ed. Clifton J. Allen, vol. 8 (Nashville: Broadman Press, 1969), p. 48.

18. John H. Hayes, and Carl R. Holiday, *Biblical Exegesis: A Beginner's Handbook* (Atlanta: John Knox Press, 1982), p. 56. This book, although not as helpful as Fee's, deals in individual chapters with form, tradition, and redaction criticism. As these critical approaches are not discussed within the limitations of this article, the reader might refer to Hayes and Holiday for an introduction to these disciplines.

19. Fee, p. 78.

20. Fee, *Exegesis,* and Hayes, *Biblical Exegesis,* give copious attention to hundreds of practical tools for biblical exegesis.

21. Eric C. Malte, "Preaching from the Greek New Testament," *Concordia Theological Monthly 25* (September 1954): 656.

22. Jesse Northcutt, "The Forks of the Road," in *Chapel Messages,* ed. H. C. Brown, Jr., and Charles P. Johnson (Grand Rapids, Mich.: Baker Book House, 1966), p. 111.

23. E. Earle Ellis, "What Good are Hebrew and Greek?" *Christianity Today* 26 (May 1972): 9.

24. Ibid.

25. Marvin R. Vincent, *Word Studies in the New Testament,* Vol. I (Grand Rapids: Wm. B. Eerdmans Publishing Co., 1946), p. xii.

26. Robinson, p. 59.

27. Brown, *Steps,* p. 56.

28. Ibid., p. 57.

29. Kenneth S. Wuest, "The Greek New Testament and Expository Preaching," *Bibliotheca Sacra* 117 (January 1960): 40–41.

30. Malte, p. 658.

31. W. A. Criswell, *The Holy Spirit in Today's World* (Grand Rapids, Mich.: Zondervan Publishing House, 1966), pp. 132–36.

32. Ronald A. Ward, *Hidden Meaning in the New Testament* (Old Tappan, New Jersey: Fleming H. Revell, 1969), p. 15.

33. Jay E. Adams, "Help in Using the Original Language in Preaching," *Journal of Pastoral Practice* 3 (1979): 169.

34. Walter C. Kaiser, Jr., *Toward an Exegetical Theology* (Grand Rapids, Mich.: Baker Book House, 1981), p. 99. See also pp. 165–81 where Kaiser gives numerous examples of syntactical displays from both Old and New Testament passages in both original languages and English. Fee, p. 61. See pp. 60–76 where Fee presents numerous examples of his "sentence flow schematic" which is equivalent to Kaiser's displays.

35. Brevard S. Childs, *The Book of Exodus,* The Old Testament Library (Philadelphia: Westminster Press, 1974), p. xv.

36. J. Daniel Baumann, *An Introduction to Contemporary Preaching* (Grand Rapids, Mich.: Baker Book House, 1972), p. 103.

37. Brown, *Southwestern Sermons,* p. 161.

38. Ibid., p. 163.

39. Ibid., p. 164.

40. Webb B. Garrison, *Creative Imagination in Preaching* (Nashville: Abingdon Press, 1960), pp. 118–31.

41. Ibid., p. 131.

NOTE

Scripture quotations in this article are from the KING JAMES VERSION of the Bible.

Pastoral Preaching

PHILIP HACKING

I have an abiding passion for what I have termed "pastoral preaching," that is, the exposition of God's Word in the context of the local church community, linking with pastoral care. I have discovered that the ministry of God's Word often evokes a sense of need and then answers that need. It is a tragedy in our day that we have lost faith in the effectiveness of this type of exposition.

The Ministry of Preaching

We have lost out on the centrality of biblical and expository ministry. We exalt worship but not preaching. There are seminars and courses on drama, dance, and the use of audio-visual aids. But with some glorious exceptions, we do not train people to preach, and indeed, we create an atmosphere in which the sermon seems almost expendable. In his book *Preaching and Preachers,* Dr. Martyn Lloyd-Jones sounds the clarion call: "Ultimately . . . to me the work of preaching is the highest and the greatest and the most glorious calling to which anyone can ever be called. If you want something in addition to that I would say without any hesitation that the most urgent need in the Christian Church is true preaching; and as it is the greatest and the most urgent need in the Church, it is obviously the greatest need of the world also."[1] True revival will come when we rediscover the power of the Word and the vitality of a consistent preaching ministry. Otherwise, growth will be exotic and transient, like the shallow soil of our Lord's parable.

Biblical preaching should produce balanced Christians. Sadly, balanced Christian living has received very bad press and almost sounds dull. Therefore, we must pack it with New Testament dynamic before too many more casualties appear.

The balance is found in the faithful exposition of God's truth. There the amazing promises of Scripture will be set in context. They may lose some of their apparently attractive extravagance, but they in turn will offer 99 blessing in greater depth. Here the warnings will be sounded as well. We shall see the miraculous at work in the pages of Scripture and rejoice in it. We shall notice long stretches of revelation with no reference to miracles at all. We shall discover the help of the Spirit and find ourselves expecting far more from Him. But we shall also note the uncomfortable commands of Scripture demanding daily discipline and obedience.

We have the perfect blueprint for church growth in the famous Jerusalem Quadrilateral of Acts 2:42. The foundation of that dynamic early church was the apostles' teaching of doctrine. The task of every Christian leader, therefore, is to unravel the mystery of the Word of God and to proclaim boldly its teaching. We live in an age when people want a direct word from the Lord apart from the authority of Scripture. Such subjective Christianity can be disastrous. Mercifully, the Lord, by His Spirit, communicates to us today, but every personal revelation must always be subservient to the revealed truth of the New Testament. Worldly publicity stunts will reap only a transitory harvest. Church history contains many illustrations of this kind of deviation from God's plan. We should build on the rock of the Word of God, for any other foundation will ultimately collapse.

The whole doctrine of the church is at stake here. As an Anglican minister I work primarily within the local church under the theological authority of the 1662 Book of Common Prayer, which defines the church as "a congregation of faithful men in which the pure Word of God is preached and the sacraments are duly ministered."[2] The centrality of the Word and its preaching is very clear. But there are always problems of emphasis. Some churches see preaching as the significant element and think of the rest of the service as mere preliminaries. However, we are in greater danger today of going to the other extreme. Praise is the order of the day. Some have even suggested that if praise is really heartfelt, then preaching is almost superfluous. We shall soon reap the whirlwind if we allow congregations to be content with singing and nothing more. Very quickly such praise becomes mindless, and the apostle Paul takes care always to point out that worship must be with the mind as well as with the Spirit. (See 1 Cor. 14:13–15.)

At the heart of all worship must be the preaching and hearing of the Word of God, without which acts of worship can rapidly become meaningless repetition. As a preacher I am happiest when the Word of God comes as the climax of a service. There are arguments for having the sermon earlier so there can be a proper response of praise and prayer. But there is great value in hearing the sermon immediately before being sent out into the world to obey. Preaching in the New Testament called for a verdict. Our Lord ended the Sermon on the Mount with the parable of the two houses and the call to hear the Word of God and do it (Matt. 7:24–27). Peter, on the day of Pentecost, was more than ready when the audience asked what they ought to do with their sense of conviction (Acts 2:37). To that end he had been preaching in the Spirit. In that way it is helpful if, after quiet reflection, those who have heard the Word go back into the world and seek to carry out its implications.

The Need for Systematic Teaching

Preacher and hearer alike should expect each sermon to be an act of God, creatively blending scriptural truth with subjective experience. Even in Old Testament days there are parallels, as in Nehemiah, chapter 8, where Ezra the scribe preaches and the people of Israel respond, aware of their sins and eager to make amends. I believe people are unconsciously crying for a word from the Lord and often come in vain to worship. The failure for that word to reach people is sometimes because the preacher has lost confidence in Scripture and sometimes because the faithful expositor does not relate the truths of Scripture to the world of today. We must be earthed at both ends. Without Scripture our comments are banal; without our feet firmly on the ground of contemporary reality we are merely biblical experts. Our aim is not to produce a congregation who simply know the Bible but a congregation who know the Lord and obey Him.

To enable the people of God to hear the Word of God there needs to be a regular teaching sequence. It is vital that people be instructed in the whole counsel of God and not just the particular themes and fads of their minister. I have always sought to teach in blocks based on individual books of the Bible, biblical themes, or biblical characters. Sometimes it is valuable to study the Lord's Prayer, the Ten Commandments, the Sermon on the Mount, or the Apostles' Creed. It is wise not to make the series too long. I believe a congregation will be the healthier if there is a structured teaching ministry, and the preacher himself will be kept from going stale with this kind of discipline.

Of course, the preacher needs to be sensitive to what is happening in the world and to be a person of imagination. Events in the outside world color people's minds as they enter to worship, and it is foolish to ignore them. From time to time some major event may call for a last minute change of sermon. More likely, by the gracious providence of God, the theme already planned for the day can incorporate a reference to an urgent event. At the same time, it is vital that the agenda for our sermons be dictated not by the world and its ideas nor even by the congregation and its desires, but by the balance of Scripture. There are many issues which I would not have dared to preach unless they had come in the sequence of teaching.

The particular challenge of preaching in worship is that inevitably there will be a glorious cross-section of levels of Christian maturity, and each one comes needing to hear a word from the Lord. Without the miracle of the Spirit at work this would be a sheer impossibility. We are wise to remember that this need is met by groups organized around common interests or levels of understanding. The recent popularity of nurture groups, or basics groups, is altogether a good thing. It encourages young Christians to meet together to receive the milk of the Word. It only becomes tragic when some people never get beyond the basics. Equally important are Bible classes for young people of various age levels. Yet there is a special value in exhorting the gathered congregation. An important part of the worship experience is the atmosphere of being assembled in the presence of God and of having prepared as a congregation through different facets of worship to receive the word of the Lord.

There is always two-way traffic in preaching. Naturally the preacher must prepare thoroughly. No amount of efficient administration can take the place of waiting upon the Lord to hear what He would say through His Word and carefully preparing that Word. Paul's exhortation to Timothy remains the classic challenge to preachers: "Preach the Word, be urgent in season and out of season, convince, rebuke, and exhort, be unfailing in patience and in teaching" (2 Tim. 4:2, RSV). Paul reminds Timothy that it is all the more necessary because of the false teaching that is prevalent, and that certainly is the clarion call of today. Those of us who love God's Word and believe in its purity must be bold and imaginative in its proclamation. The truth needs to be heard loud and clear.

The other side of the two-way traffic in preaching is the need for the congregation to prepare prayerfully. There is a grace of listening and there is a discipline in taking God's Word seriously. For some people it means taking notes in the sermon in order to help concentration. For others it may mean following a series through by listening to taped sermons. Supremely, it calls for an attitude of mind which expects that God will speak. In many cases this thirst for the truth from the congregation can lift a preacher to a new level. I am happy to report that this is my normal lot in my own congregation, and it makes preaching a sheer delight.

The Ministry of Evangelism

Alongside my passion for pastoral preaching is my involvement in the ministry of evangelism. Indeed they are two sides of the same coin. It has been my privilege to be involved in many evangelistic missions around Great Britain. There are many methods and arenas of evangelism, but I believe evangelism within the local church is of particular value. You have there the perfect preparation and follow-up system. But whatever the method, at the center must be proclamation.

The whole Christ is to be proclaimed. This will inevitably mean some concentration of the message, as in the *kerygma* (the condensed essentials of the gospel) of the Acts of the Apostles. The early chapters of that book are well worth studying to see how Peter and the others concentrated the message on the person, the death, the resurrection, and the coming again of Jesus. All are linked with the Pentecost experience of the Spirit. The story of the birth of the church in Samaria in Acts chapter 8 is very instructive. It all started with the gossiping of the gospel by those who were scattered through the persecution following the death of Stephen, and then Philip the preacher came with a message that drew in the gospel net. In such a way the whole church today should be involved in the life-giving proclamation.

Evangelism is often rendered ineffective by our failure to teach young Christians, and often indeed the motive for evangelism is lost because the Word is not taught faithfully.

Our Lord Himself is the greatest evangelist. To see Him in action is the best training you will ever find. Watch Him deal with people in the gospel accounts and notice His sensitivity and His great blend of grace and truth. He remains as well the greatest example of a teacher, and we do well to study His teaching ministry in light of the church's work today.

In the New Testament evangelism and teaching always go hand in hand. At the end of Matthew's gospel, Jesus urged the disciples to go make 103

disciples and to teach (Matt. 28:19–20). It is often difficult to differenti-
ate between evangelism and teaching, for many people have come to new
life through the teaching ministry of the church. When the apostle Paul
preached the good news, he would regularly debate, dialogue, or even
argue with the religious people of his day. Although we live in a very
different society with much less open discussion of God and Scripture, it
is still vital that the mind be reached in proclaiming Christ. In Romans
6:17 Paul reminds us that all parts of the personality are involved in the
conversion experience: the will, the mind, and the heart—the emotions.
Evangelism must appeal to all three. There is a kind of decisionism practiced today which challenges the will without much content. There is also
a great deal of emotionalism, which can create a very superficial response. Or there can be a cerebral presentation of the gospel which
never gets beyond the intellect. The whole person must be involved.

If that is true at the beginning of the Christian experience, it is equally
true in its continuance. Paul is adamant about the importance of edifying
and upbuilding the church. This stands out most of all in 1 Corinthians
chapters 12 and 14, where he is discussing the place of the gifts of the
Spirit. Paul takes great pains to emphasize that the use of the gifts should
be for edification and upbuilding. This is why he discourages excessive
enthusiasm for the gift of tongues in public worship and encourages the
gift of prophecy. Argument will rage about the exact meaning of prophecy
in Paul's writings and what it means for the church today. I believe it to be
more than preaching, but no preaching worthy of the name should be less
than prophetic. It is possible to expound Scripture without any prophetic
word for today. However, we are not out to create learned theologians, but
born again, mature Christians. There is a place for a more spontaneous
word from the Lord, but it should always be judged by Scripture (see
1 Cor. 14:29). The aim of the prophetic word must always be to build
people up into maturity.

The Teaching Ministry in the Church

We need systematic teaching in order that the people of God might
grow and relate their faith to everyday life. After Barnabas had established the church at Antioch, he brought the apostle Paul there for a whole
year to teach and edify the faithful. It could be argued that the greatest
need of our day is for that kind of teaching.

The church's teaching program is much more than a pulpit ministry. Much teaching takes place outside the worship service, and all who teach should themselves be well instructed. It is nothing less than tragic when we consider how lightly we have treated the teaching ministry of the church. So often our Sunday schools have produced utterly ill-informed young people who are delighted when they can finally throw off the shackles of Sunday School! Of course, there are glorious exceptions, and some of us rejoice that we were well taught. Yet all too often our Sunday schools are the Cinderellas of the church's life. We assume that anyone can look after the children, and it is almost as bad with young people. We often assume that children and young people simply want to be entertained. But here are young minds in formative stages! We should set our sights high.

I believe we should never teach children anything that they must unlearn when they grow up. In an odd kind of way I have always believed that to bring up children on the myth of Father Christmas is to put them in danger of equating Jesus with that figure, whom adults reject as childish myth. Children can learn profound truths at their own levels and often have deeper faith than many questioning adults.

The groups within the church ought not to be just occasions for fellowship and sharing but also places of learning. There has been an overemphasis on sharing: focusing on ourselves and our problems and experiences. There is a place for this kind of openness, but it is a very unhealthy norm for group work. Rather, as we learn together we deepen and open ourselves more to the Lord and His truths and to one another.

Every minister or Christian leader should make planning the preaching and teaching in Sunday worship a priority. During the summer holidays I always look ahead to the whole year and seek to find a balanced pattern of teaching. I believe that if the preacher is planning and is excited about the truth, he will probably carry the congregation with him. If he seems to be always rushing at the last minute with some thought for the day he will produce fairly thin and immature Christians.

The High Calling of a Preacher

I have never forgotten my ordination and the Bible I received as a symbol of my new ministry and as a mark of the authority under which I was to work. At the Reformation this was one of the great revolutions. No more did the priest receive a chalice as a symbol of his ministry, but rather the Scriptures. That revolution took the church back to the biblical perspective. But this can be an idle piece of ceremony unless all who minister are constantly aware that they are under the authority of the Word of God. It is frightening to prepare messages week by week and to recognize that it is impossible to preach with integrity unless the preacher himself is subject to the truth. I always find great comfort in Jeremiah. In spite of his occasional rebellion, he trembled at the Word and at the same time had that fire in his belly which could not be contained.

It is a privilege to counsel would-be ministers. I always inquire on two levels as to their sense of passion. In the first place I seek to discover whether there is a passion for the Word of God. The potential preacher may have had little scope for preaching, but at least there ought to be a deep desire to communicate that Word to others. Secondly, I inquire about a passion for souls. The phrase may be somewhat archaic, but the reality should always be fresh. A minister must love people and love the Word. It is possible for someone to enjoy the Word of God, but to be utterly aloof. It is equally possible for people to be caring and loving but have no word from the Lord. Neither of these would make true ministers of the gospel. In our age we should look not for more ministers but for those who have this double passion. It would not take too many of such people to transform the church radically.

There is a certain danger in being in a position of proclaiming the truth with dogmatic assurance. Normally the preacher is not questioned, and indeed it is arguable that the Word of God is not to be discussed but obeyed. Therefore, the preacher must have a stern self-discipline. The pulpit is not the place to throw out ideas and theories or to speak dogmatically on issues on which the Bible does not speak clearly. Then the congregation will rightly become restive, since they can disagree with an equal Christian mind and have no place to argue the toss. Of course, there is a place for seminars and discussions on controversial issues. But the teaching ministry of the Word of God has such an authority that the preacher himself must have already responded to the Word. He would be wise to speak much more in the first person than the second person when preaching. Because there is great power in the proclamation, there is great need for responsible use of it. I suppose that one of the great safeguards is a knowledge of people and a love for them. The sermon does not stand in isolation but it is all part and parcel of a pastoral ministry.

But teaching does not begin and end in the pulpit. There is a great principle in the New Testament of instructing others who will continue the good work. So our Lord spent a great deal of His precious time instructing rather reluctant disciples in the truth so that they might be equipped to continue the work when He had gone. In his second letter to Timothy, Paul expresses a very great principle: "What you have heard from me before many witnesses entrust to faithful men who will be able to teach others also" (2 Tim. 2:2 RSV). You see the sequence? Paul—Timothy—faithful men—others. In this way the work is multiplied. It could well be that, in the days when people did listen to sermons and preachers did preach with conviction, the church did not train others to communicate the gospel message. That principle should be written deep in the strategies of every local church.

Much teaching of this kind is very personal. I believe small groups and one-to-one ministry and counseling should always have a high place in the work of the church, but we must beware of making a god of counseling. I am sometimes deemed heretical for my view that the success of a sermon is measured not by how many people stay to be counseled but by how few. Very often if the Word has been preached clearly it is a matter between the individual and the Lord. All is clear and the person is able to sort it out himself or herself. Of course, this is simplistic, and there will always be issues that need to be talked over with a mature Christian friend. In my experience, however, people stay for counseling because they are bewildered, not because we have brought home the challenge of the gospel in the power of the Spirit. Some of the most effective meetings have been followed by a quiet going home, to put right what God has clearly said to us.

The Work of the Spirit

In Scripture there is always a balance between the Word and the Spirit. Right from the first chapter of Genesis, they work hand in hand, as "God said . . ." and "the Spirit of God was moving on the face of the waters" (Gen. 1:2 RSV). On the day of Pentecost the Spirit came, the crowds were drawn by the praising of God in tongues, and then Peter preached. After the preaching, thousands were converted and the Spirit moved afresh. In the home of Cornelius, Peter was still in the middle of expounding the truth when the Spirit fell upon Cornelius and the household. We are to be 107 true to the Word, and then the Spirit will drive home its message in individual lives. It is not unlike the moment in the Old Testament when Elijah was contesting with the false prophets. After he had made all the preparation that was necessary and had prayed, then the fire fell. Only God can bring the fire; only we can do the preparation. An ill-prepared sermon should not expect the fire to fall, and a sermon studiously prepared without prayer may be beautiful and eloquent, but quite dead.

What God has joined together, sadly men have often put asunder. Some of us major on the Word and are very fearful of the Spirit. We are true to Scripture but expect nothing to happen. We have good doctrine but no life. Other churches today major on the Spirit with little exposition of Scripture. I believe this to be a very dangerous condition in the church. There is a heart-cry for teaching, and because of the renewed interest in the Spirit the devil has found a niche by encouraging Christians to play down the need for doctrine and teaching. There is no monopoly of the Spirit's work. Word and Spirit must go together. With healthy teaching and expectation of the Spirit's work in that context, we shall have mature Christians. They will not be like children who are tossed to and fro by every latest religious fad, and they will not be stale and prematurely old in the faith. When the Spirit is at work, we are being constantly renewed and are growing younger spiritually every day.

All of us who care about these great themes must look to the future and trust God to do yet greater things. It is a call to those of us who minister to set a worthy example and to encourage a younger generation to follow in the same footsteps in which we have followed. As the apostle Paul looked to the future, he knew how much he depended upon the younger generation to take up the challenge. So he brings his exhortation to Timothy with a challenge to "preach the word" (2 Tim. 4:2). The command suggests a very definite commitment. It will be an ongoing work, but every now and again the Christian minister must renew his commitment to make this proclamation the priority of his life. That is one of the greatest needs for today. There can be no substitute for dynamic, convincing proclamation of the truth.

NOTES

1. Martyn Lloyd-Jones, *Preaching and Preachers* (London: Hodder and Stoughton, 1971).
2. Episcopal Church, *The Book of Common Prayer and Administration of the Sacraments and Other Rites and Ceremonies of the Church* (New York: Church Hymnal Corp., 1979).

   Scripture quotations in this article are from the REVISED STANDARD VERSION of the Bible. Copyright © 1946, 1952, 1971, 1973.

The Art of Preaching as an Act of Worship

PAUL S. REES

In seventy years of preaching there have been relatively few of my colleagues with whom I have had repeated and extended discussions of the preaching vocation. Of these few, I might add, most have been promoted from proclamation on earth to celebration in glory.

Among those who are "yet alive to see each other's face" is my highly esteemed friend, Stephen Olford. Whether in England, Ireland, the United States, or the Far East we have had a slew of conversations on what is to us an incomparable theme: preaching the "unsearchable riches of Christ," expounding the eternal Word of the living God.

The first time I heard Dr. Olford preach, now more than thirty years ago, he was pastor of a thriving Baptist church in the Richmond suburb of metropolitan London. The carefully wrought outline and structure of the sermon, the close correlation between the headings of his message and the content of the passage he was expounding, together with the flaming vigor of his spirit, made me realize that here was a prophet of God for whom the preaching vocation, far from being a mere profession, was in fact a holy passion. Time has amply confirmed my initial assessment. The years may have whitened Dr. Olford's hair, but they have done nothing to diminish his ardor.

Furthermore, my friend holds preaching in such high regard that his incessant concern about the quality of his own sermons has been projected to include an eagerness to see the level of preaching raised among all, both young and old, who have heard the Pauline summons to "preach the Word."

For this reason—and others—I deem it a privilege to contribute to this highly deserved recognition of Stephen Olford, preacher extraordinary.

The Art of Preaching as an Act of Worship

No sermon, however homiletically artistic, is ever complete if considered solely as an individual effort by the preacher. It is the congregational context, as well as the sermonic content, that must be taken into account.

The subject is worship. The issue is homiletics versus liturgics. While some Protestant groups have been far out on the rim of this debate, others have been fervently involved. Shall we revive liturgy in order to enrich worship? Or, as some would prefer to put it, shall we enrich liturgy in order to enhance worship? This is not the place to explore the ramifications of the debate. It is the place, however, to point out—and to protest against—a false antithesis. Granted that in evangelical Protestantism, particularly of the "free church" variety, the tendency has been to misconstrue and undervalue those forms of congregational prayer and praise which precede the sermon. In this distorted perspective we tend to look upon these exercises and offerings as "preliminaries." The word should be an offense to us. The abandonment of its absurdity cannot be too swift.

But now an opposite peril threatens. Protestants, we are told, have become a sermon-tasting breed who, whether fascinated by a pulpit star or bored by a homiletical hack, are strangers to the art, the beauty, the dignity, the sacramental mysticism of worship. On the whole, those who exalt ritual denigrate preaching. Whether by accident or design, it is generally true that the heavily liturgical service is the service of the ten-to-twelve-minute sermon. Again, the numerous facts and facets of the present discussion are beyond the range of our purpose. The extremists in both camps can ill afford to be unteachable. What one deplores is the fallacy of fancying the sermon as something apart from worship. It is implied—and occasionally declared—that in the liturgy God is acting, while in the preaching it is man.

This is dangerously opaque thinking, the corrective answer to which is the following series of insights:

Preaching Is a Redemptive Event

"True preaching," says Dr. Donald G. Miller in *Fire in Thy Mouth*, "is an extension of the Incarnation into the contemporary moment, the transfiguration of the Cross and the Resurrection from ancient facts of a remote past into living realities of the present."[1] What we have in authentic preaching is not a repetition of Calvary (since that is unrepeatable) but a contemporizing of it. The Scriptures having dependably recorded it, the Holy Spirit now dynamically affirms it; and in the preacher, if he be the man of God he should be, both the record and the affirmation find a claiming voice. This makes the sermon vastly more than something said; it is something *done*. It is the saving, healing, strengthening God in action through his servant for the people. To separate this from a church's worship experience is perilous nonsense.

Preaching, Moreover, Is Actually a Congregational Function

In an essay entitled "Preaching as Worship" the scintillating theologian of a generation ago, Peter T. Forsythe, observes that "true preaching presupposes a church, and not merely a public." Reading this, my own mind leaped back to Peter's sermon on the day of Pentecost. The account begins with the revealing statement, "But Peter, standing up with the eleven, said . . ." (Acts 2:14). The proclamation of the gospel to an unbelieving "public" was made in the context of a believing "church."

Furthermore, it will be seen that in Peter's preaching that day the church was preaching. A New Testament sermon, far from being a parade of the opinions of a man with a clerical title, should be in effect the congregation witnessing to its faith—both for its own edification and for the persuasion of those who were without faith. It is the congregation "hearing their one hope," not with "an empty wonder" but with illuminated adoration, not "sadly contented with a show of things" but discontented with anything through which the eternal is failing to show.

To say that such preaching does not have in it the dimension of worship is to be under a strange illusion.

Preaching, We Should Not Hesitate to Say, Has a Sacramental Character

Not sacerdotal, mind you, but sacramental! A sermon is not a communication of grace in which the transmission is guaranteed by the insignia of the office of preacher. On the other hand, the sermon is indeed the visible and audible sign of the grace that is given when, to borrow the language of the epistle to the Hebrews, "the word preached" is "mixed with faith" on the part of those who hear (Heb. 4:2). The pulpit should be seen as a sign of the grace of God standing within the divinely created community of faith—the church.

When I was a young preacher I read something by the Archbishop of

Canterbury, William Temple, that has lived with me across these several decades:

> For worship is the submission of all our nature to God. It is the quickening of conscience by His holiness; the nourishment of mind with His truth; the purifying of imagination by His beauty; the opening of the heart to His love; the surrender of will to His purpose; and all of this gathered up in adoration, the most selfless emotion of which our nature is capable, and therefore, the chief remedy for that self-centeredness which is our original sin and the source of all actual sin.[2]

Surely that person holds too low a view of preaching who doubts that it can contribute magnificently to the worthy ends so eloquently described by Archbishop Temple.

A further insight is this: *preaching is an oblation*. My Webster gives, as one definition of oblation, "something offered in worship." So be it! An authentic sermon qualifies.

An authentic sermon is an offering of *prayer*. The preacher's? Yes. And the congregation's too. A sermon not steeped in prayer is unworthy of the name.

It is an offering of the *intellect*. Read Paul in 1 Corinthians 14 on the relation between prophesying and intelligibility. As John Stott says tersely, "The mind matters." Preaching is seriously flawed if it consists of little more than an entertaining engagement of the emotions.

It is an offering of the *will*—first the preacher's and then the congregation's. Whether the sermon is about the gift of eternal life, the summons to holy living, the practice of stewardship, the life of prayer, or the lordship of Christ over our attitudes on race, money, sex, and war, it brings the hearers to some "valley of decision" in which the response is Yes or No or, at the least, Not yet.

A lecture may feed the mind or titillate the emotions; a sermon, while doing both, is distinctively a call to action. It confronts the will.

A sermon is, in Forsythe's unforgettable phrase, "the organized Hallelujah" of the church, joyously confessing its faith in the gospel, obediently submitting to its claims.

If such an offering is not worship, then nothing is!

NOTES

1. Donald G. Miller, *Fire in Thy Mouth* (Nashville: Abingdon Press, 1954).
2. William Temple, *Readings in St. John's Gospel* (Toronto: Macmillan, 1939), p. 68.
   Scripture quotations in this article are from the KING JAMES VERSION of the Bible.

The Theologian and the Evangelist

In 1966 a World Congress on Evangelism was held in Berlin, West Germany. The honorary chairman of that gathering was evangelist Billy Graham, and the acting chairman was Dr. Carl F. H. Henry, the noted American theologian and editor of *Christianity Today*.

At the opening session of the congress Dr. Henry introduced Mr. Graham to the delegates by saying something like this: "Several years ago after Billy Graham graduated from Wheaton College, I urged him to go on to seminary. Fortunately, Billy did not take my advice. Had he done so, we might have lost the most effective evangelist of our generation."

While Dr. Henry, the distinguished scholar, made that comment with a touch of jest, educators sitting in the audience shifted uneasily in their seats. Theological education and evangelism have too often made an oil-and-water mix. Noted evangelists of the last two centuries suspect that seminary graduates have emptied the churches by degrees, and the slip of the tongue that turns *seminary* into *cemetery* has strong Freudian overtones.

Yet this antagonism between theology and evangelism developed in recent history. Theological scholarship came under suspicion when it was infected by German criticism. During the past two hundred years the most savage attacks made on the historic Christian faith have come from professing Christians. German critics starting with Bruno Bauer and fortified by the agnostic philosophy of Immanuel Kant and the idealism of Georg Friedrich Hegel, produced rationalism. These scholars wrote off evangelical Christianity as outmoded and out of step with the times. They devoted their brilliant intellects and sharpened pens to ripping apart the pages of Scripture. They took the miracles out of history, the fire out of hell, the deity away from Jesus, and left the Bible in shreds. The Old Testament was dismissed as fables about a tribal god and the New Testament docu-

115

ments were treated like old letters from a distant time stored in the attic of religion.

German criticism arose at the same time that changes took place in American theological education. Before the Revolutionary War young men prepared for the ministry by living in the homes of older ministers. The younger and older men would study the Bible together, read theology, discuss church history, and then move about the parish visiting the sick and instructing families.

While this initial approach to theological education had the obvious advantage of keeping the theoretical and practical together, it had serious problems. Not all the older ministers could provide the breadth of training the younger pastors needed. Gradually, church leaders felt the need for more consistent education for the clergy, and they turned to the colleges to provide it. Seminaries emerged first as graduate schools of religion. Those who taught in them were selected because of their education. Professors in the schools were enamored with the latest scholarship that came from the continent, and the critical views taught in the classroom filtered down through the students to the churches.

Unfortunately, seminaries were seldom held accountable to local congregations. The schools received handsome endowments from wealthy individuals or denominations, and as a result, scholars did not pay much attention to what their teaching did to the churches. If men and women in the pews felt they were drinking from a muddy stream, they were powerless to clean up the spiritual pollution.

The Divorce of Theology and Evangelism

Theologians in the seminaries often belittled evangelism. Evangelists were dismissed as unscholarly, noisy nuisances. Many in the churches, on the other side, reacted against seminaries and scholarship. In their eyes, theology appeared both unnecessary and dangerous. Revivals under evangelists like Charles Finney, Dwight L. Moody, Sam Jones, Bob Jones, and Billy Sunday—all theologically uneducated—brought into the church converts who saw little need for ministers with seminary training. For them, evangelism stood as the only need of the hour, and at the turn of the twentieth century Bible institutes were founded that minimized theology and put their emphasis on practical training. The rise of faith missions heightened the place of evangelism. Without doubt, the Bible institutes and faith missions provided a needed correction within the church, but often at the price of theological reflection.

What is more, members of the scholarly community had reason to suspect evangelists. Some were little more than irresponsible sensationalists more concerned with nickels and numbers than with people. When Sinclair Lewis wrote *Elmer Gantry,* he pointed to a disgraceful condition in which some evangelists manipulated their congregations and, in the name of God, fleeced them instead of feeding them. Throughout large sections of the country, people looked forward to the circus and the revival as the major community events of the year. In fact, the two had much in common. Both were held in tents and both attracted the entire community. At times the only observable difference was that at the circus you paid for the entertainment before you entered the tent, while in the revival your money was collected inside the tent. Many evangelists entered the ministry with little more than a sensational life story and ten sermons and kept on the move to preach them to different crowds. Education was suspect. "If a little knowledge is a dangerous thing," they reasoned, "how much more dangerous would a lot of learning be?"

The separation of theology and evangelism proved a tragic divorce. The evangelist and the theologian are both needed today. Evangelism without sound doctrine decays into ignorant fanaticism. Theology without the goal of making converts degenerates into cold intellectualism. The result of this separation is a faith that is neither intellectually or biblically sound nor spiritually satisfying. The people of God need to appreciate both the theologian and the evangelist.

A Theological Evangelist and an Evangelistic Theologian

We can observe both callings at work in two outstanding leaders of the eighteenth-century church. John Wesley was an evangelist. He was born into a religious home. Yet only as an adult was he converted to Christ. After studying for the ministry at Oxford, Wesley traveled to the United States as a missionary to the American Indians. Discouraged with his efforts, he returned home to England. One evening Wesley was invited to attend a religious meeting at Aldersgate, where he listened to the reading of Martin Luther's preface to the book of Romans. In those moments Wesley felt his heart "strangely warmed" and through that experience became truly converted.

117

John Wesley plunged into an exhausting evangelistic ministry. Preaching two to five sermons a day, he preached at least forty thousand sermons in his lifetime. In order to reach his countrymen with the gospel, he traveled over two hundred fifty thousand miles on horseback. His ministry produced lasting effects. Not only did he change the face of religion in England, but according to Woodrow Wilson, he changed the whole course of English history! He opened new religious societies, administered discipline, raised vast sums of money for the poor, founded the first tract society, and engaged in controversy for the faith. At his death, he left behind one hundred thirty-five thousand communicants and five hundred preachers for the Methodist church.

Wesley was born in 1703. In that same year, on the other side of the Atlantic, another man was born whose life greatly affected the church. Jonathan Edwards was a scholar. Like Wesley, he was a child of a parsonage and was the grandson of Solomon Stoddard, a noted New England Puritan minister. Edwards possessed a brilliant mind. At six, he mastered Latin; at nine he wrote a treatise on materialism; at twelve he produced an essay on spiders that is still considered biologically accurate. At thirteen he entered Yale and at seventeen graduated with highest honors.

Many of Edwards' sermons reflect his massive intellect. His works *Freedom of the Will* and *A History of Redemption* rank as classics of Christian theology. Just before his death at age fifty-five, Jonathan Edwards accepted the presidency of Princeton College. His scholarship left a lasting impression on America. Barrett Wendell, a Unitarian literary critic, named Edwards as one of three outstanding thinkers of the United States. Yale University has republished his works in honor of his contributions.

The Need for Scholars and Evangelists

Both John Wesley and Jonathan Edwards were gifts from God to the church. The people of God need scholars who can think God's thoughts after Him and evangelists who can proclaim that message clearly. If the church is to carry out Christ's commission, however, we need to go beyond a simple appreciation of both. We need a band of men and women who are theological and evangelistic theologians.

John Wesley and Jonathan Edwards combined both offices. As Wesley rode his two hundred fifty thousand miles on horseback, he produced grammars of English, French, Latin, Greek, and Hebrew. He edited a Greek New Testament and made his own translation of the Bible. His sermons and journals contain the major planks of a systematic theology. Jonathan Edwards, the scholar, became a major force in evangelism and revival. His sermon *Sinners in the Hands of An Angry God,* preached many times throughout New England, was the opening trumpet in "The Great Awakening." His unrelenting logic, his identification with the feelings of his congregation, and his use of Scripture shook his hearers out of complacency. Through him hundreds awoke to their desperate need for Jesus Christ.

The Good Marriage of Theology and Evangelism

Throughout history, effective evangelists have studied theology and strong theologians have involved themselves in evangelism. No one would question the zeal of the apostle Paul for evangelism. Under the inspiration of God he wrote to his friends in Rome, "I speak the truth in Christ—I lie not—I am ready to be anathema from Christ—to suffer eternal punishment and lose all that really matters to me—if only my people Israel could be saved!" Yet Paul was also a splendid theologian. Think of his letters to the Romans, the Ephesians, and Galatians, and you marvel at the range and depth of thought. His epistles, written in the heat of his ministry, are the quarry in which most subsequent Christian thinkers have been content to dig. In Paul theology and evangelism embraced each other. Paul became a theologian because he desired to evangelize, and theology formed the basis of his message.

Augustine, the brilliant fifth-century theologian, shaped and directed Christian thought for centuries after him, but his greatest work, *The City of God,* was motivated by a spirit of evangelism. When men and women despaired as they witnessed the collapse of Roman civilization, Augustine pointed them to the city whose builder and maker is God.

In the sixteenth century John Calvin stands out as one of the most successful evangelists in church history. This brilliant theologian not only evangelized the city of Geneva and the cantons of French-speaking Switzerland, but he became an evangelist of Europe spreading the evangelical faith from Scotland to Transylvania. Five times during his lifetime he revised his *Institutes of the Christian Religion* to achieve a clearer, more 119 convincing explanation of Christian theology in order that his followers could be more effective evangelists.

William Carey (1761–1834), the pioneer of modern overseas missions, carried the burden of Christless millions heavy on his heart. While he longed to bring the gospel to the world, his brethren, operating out of a stifling theology, were inclined to do nothing. For that reason, Carey himself, while still a country pastor, learned Hebrew, Greek, Dutch, French, and Italian. Then, driven by his concern for the lost, he traveled to India where he lapped up language after language, exploring the richness of Indian literature and, still more, sharing the treasures of Christ in the gospel. Carey established a publishing house and founded a great college—the first of its kind in India and a center of theological education in the subcontinent.

Francis Schaeffer challenged the assumptions of thousands of men and women caught up in the ferment of our times. While exposing the futility of pagan philosophy, he has argued for the sufficiency of biblical truth as a foundation for life. Francis Schaeffer, however, considered himself an evangelist whose major purpose in life lay in bringing bewildered people to a knowledge of the Savior.

Certainly there are scholars who lack spiritual fire but that is not the fault of theology. Men and women like that would be dull no matter what they did. Superficiality is not a necessary part of evangelism, and in fact, clear theology is basic to sound witness.

The Aims of the Evangelist

The first aim of an evangelist is to proclaim to the world the good news about Jesus Christ. Obviously, that requires an understanding of the message. What does it mean to believe on the Lord Jesus Christ? Is that the same as saying, "Let Jesus come into your heart," "Open your life to Christ," or "Make Jesus Lord of your life?" If we read "The blood of Jesus Christ, God's Son, cleanses us from all sin," what does that mean to the individual in the marketplace? How do you explain that truth in terms unchurched people comprehend? Take that biblical assertion apart and you are working with theology.

Sometimes what we call deep is simply muddy. Only if we understand the gospel ourselves can we hope to make it clear to others. Theology clarifies our thought, sets what Christians believe in contrast to false doctrine, and helps us make the message clear to outsiders.

A second purpose of the evangelist is to help converts develop into mature Christians. People professing faith in Christ often do not continue in the faith because they do not grow. Only the strong meat of Christian doctrine produces healthy Christians, and we never get very far as Christians without first understanding the great truths revealed to us by God in Scripture and then in faith applying them to life.

The Heart of the Scholar

If theology is basic to evangelism, evangelism is vital to theology. God's truth demands proclamation as well as study. If we propose to be Christians, then we must get on with Christ's business. Napoleon's lieutenants carried in their jackets, close to their hearts, a map of the world. World conquest was their purpose because it was Napoleon's purpose. For that they fought, sacrificed, suffered, and died. Christian scholarship exists to serve Christ's people in the world.

There is a story about Jerome, the scholar who translated the Scriptures into Latin. He was a theologian and philosopher, a grammarian who mastered Hebrew, Greek, and Latin. Like all students, Jerome loved his books. In his sleep one night, he dreamed he stood before the judgment seat of Christ:

> "Who are you?" said the Lord on the throne.
> "Jerome, a Christian," was the reply.
> "That is false," said the stern voice from the throne. "You are not a lover of Christ, but of Cicero, for where your treasure is, there your heart is also!"

Jerome awoke in a cold sweat and fell to his knees to beg forgiveness for being so in love with his manuscripts that he forgot the men and women for whom Christ died. As much as we love books, we must love Christ and people more. The evangelist needs the scholar, and the scholar needs the evangelist. Even more, the church needs scholarly evangelists and evangelistic scholars—men and women who love God not only with heart and soul, but mind as well.

C. I. Scofield was a noted pastor in Dallas, Texas, and the original 121 editor of the Scofield Bible. During 1918 he suffered a serious illness that gave him an opportunity to evaluate his ministry. In January 1919 at the opening of a new year, he wrote a letter to many of the Bible teachers he knew. One of those to whom he wrote was Dr. William Pettingill.

> Dear and Honored Brother:
> You and I are Bible teachers. It is of God's grace, and it is a great gift. But near to it is a great danger.
> For many months I have, through physical disability, been laid aside from all oral ministry. During this time, it has been increasingly laid upon me that I should beg the forbearance of my teaching brethren while I state in plain truth the teacher's danger.
> In a word, it is the neglect of the Gospel message to the unsaved. But, brother, *that* is the great *message*. It is sweet and needful to feed the flock of Christ, but it is to seek and save lost men and women that Jesus came, died, and rose again. It is not enough to repeat Gospel texts and say, "Come to Jesus." There is a *tender* seeking note in the gospel truly preached. How many gospel sermons did you preach in 1918? How many found salvation under your ministry? Let us make 1919 a mighty tireless effort to save lost men.
>
> Yours in Christ's Love,
C. I. Scofield

Let us carry on that resolve! God give us loving minds and thinking hearts. If we cannot be scholarly evangelists, then by God's grace, determine to be evangelistic scholars.

NOTE

Scripture quotations in this article are the author's own translation.

The Power of Preaching

STEPHEN F. OLFORD

N|o one can read the New Testament without being impressed by the effectiveness of the preaching of the early church. The apostles preached with supernatural power. As F. D. Coggan puts it:

> The infant Church was multiplied out of all recognition by a single sermon. By preaching, a fellowship was formed which astounded the world by its demonstration of love, which held together in community men and women of different races and conflicting backgrounds. The modern preacher is compelled to question his own heart, as he faces the astounding success of the apostolic preaching.[1]

The answer to this serious question requires a broader treatment than we can comprehend in one lecture. So we must, of necessity, restrict ourselves to one passage of Scripture. Among the many that we could select, I have chosen the first five verses of 1 Corinthians, chapter 2. In simple and succinct terms, the apostle Paul here reveals that the power of evangelistic preaching is related to the message of the preacher, the manner of the preacher, and the motive of the preacher. Let us consider these three aspects of our subject with the prayer that God will inspire us, as well as instruct us, in the art and act of evangelistic proclamation. First:

Proclamation Is Related to the Message of the Preacher

"And I, brethren, when I came to you, came not with excellency of speech or of wisdom, declaring unto you the testimony of God. For I determined not to know any thing among you, save Jesus Christ, and him crucified" (vv. 1–2).

We cannot examine these words in their context without discovering that the power of preaching was inherent in the very message Paul proclaimed. And it is not difficult to arrive at what was the content of his message. According to our text, it might be stated as follows:

123

The Message of True Preaching Is the Person of Christ

"For I determined not to know any thing among you, save Jesus Christ" (v. 2).

In 1936 Professor C. H. Dodd wrote a book entitled *The Apostolic Preaching and Its Development.* According to A. M. Hunter this book is "one of the most important and positive contributions to New Testament science in our generation."[2] And I may add that it will more than repay the prayerful and careful perusal of preachers of the gospel. In this work, Dodd points out that the central message of apostolic preaching was the person and work of the Lord Jesus Christ. He amplifies this by showing that there were five main emphases in the *kerygma.* The first emphasis was on the fulfillment of the Old Testament Scriptures in relation to the coming of the Messiah. The second emphasis was on the earthly life of Jesus. The third emphasis was on the death of Christ. The fourth emphasis was on the resurrection and exaltation of the Savior, and the fifth and last emphasis was on repentance toward God and faith in our Lord Jesus Christ—in the light of coming judgment.

Dr. Coggan has made a similar study in his book, *The Ministry of the Word,* where he reveals that each of the four main words employed in the Acts of the Apostles to describe the activity of Christian preaching has as its object "Jesus," "Jesus Christ," "the Lord Jesus," "Jesus and the resurrection," "peace through Christ," "the word of the Lord," and so on.[3] It is clear, therefore, that the central message of apostolic preaching was the person of our Lord Jesus Christ.

This was not only true of the apostles but also of the Lord Jesus Christ Himself. As one German theologian has phrased it, "Jesus Christ the Son of God knew no greater task than to point men and women to Himself." To support this, we might quote Professor R.V.G. Tasker who says:

> The prime duty of the Christian preacher is not to bid men to undertake the impossible task of solving their social and economic problems in the light of the Sermon on the Mount, but to call them to repent and to submit to the rule of God. For Jesus, it is clear, was not an expounder of a noble system of ethics, nor a reformer of society, but a proclaimer of God's will, in obedience to which He Himself lived, spoke, suffered and died.[4]

Now the point in stressing the centrality of Christ in our preaching is simply that Jesus Himself is "the power of God, and the wisdom of God," as Paul makes plain in this very epistle (1:24). Only as we make Christ our message does preaching become powerful. There is little to encourage us to believe that God will bless our sermons, our homiletics, or our oratory. But we can be sure that when we preach Christ, the Spirit of power will overshadow us.

My father, who was a missionary for many years in Angola, West Africa, used to recall an important lesson he learned during the days of his training. Studying under a famous evangelist who took his students out on field work, he was puzzled again and again by the seeming lack of response to the powerful preaching of this man of God. One night he approached the evangelist on this matter. He said, "I cannot understand it. The place was packed with people. The power of God was present to save, and yet so few answered the call to repentance and faith." The old man paused for a moment, then with a smile made this statement: "Young man, the salvation in human lives is the sovereign work of God. We must leave the results to Him. Our task is to preach Christ and Him crucified." And then he added: "And remember this: God is always pleased to hear His Son well spoken of."

In my judgment, this is precisely what Paul means when he says, "I determined not to know any thing among you, save Jesus Christ, and him crucified" (v. 2).

God make us like John Wesley who could say again and again, as he traveled across England: "I offered Christ to the people."[5]

But with the message of the person of Christ, notice that:

The Message of True Preaching Is the Passion of Christ

"For I determined not to know any thing among you, save Jesus Christ, and him crucified" (v. 2).

As one commentator puts it: "We can scarcely realise [in our day] the stumbling block which the preaching of a crucified Christ must have been to Jews and Greeks, the enormous temptation to keep the cross in the background which the early teachers would naturally have felt, and the sublime and confident faith which must have nerved St. Paul to make it the central fact of all his teaching."[6] And yet the apostle knew from the Scriptures, as well as from personal experience, that the preaching of the cross constituted "the power of God" (1:18). It is the cross of Christ which expresses the divine mind, which reveals the divine estimate of human sin, which exhibits the divine love, and yet does all this on a hu- 125 man platform, so that we are enabled to appreciate the mystery of the heavenly counsels. Although the cross is a stumbling block to the religionist and a laughingstock to the rationalist, it is nonetheless the power of God to those that are saved. Only in the cross of Christ is man's only hope displayed and offered. There is something irresistibly attractive about the message of the cross. Jesus said, "And I, if I be lifted up from the earth, will draw all men unto me" (John 12:32).

What is more, there can never be a Pentecost in our preaching before there is a Calvary in our preaching. As the Moravians used to put it, "The Spirit always answers to the blood."

Dr. Billy Graham recalls the story of how he preached in one of our great outdoor stadiums on one occasion and sensed a deadness, not only in his message but in the whole meeting. On his way back to the hotel that night, he was accompanied by a well-known layman. As they talked together, Billy Graham shared his experience with this businessman who immediately countered with this remark: "I agree with you, there was no power in that service tonight, and apparently little blessing, and I think I know the reason," added the gentleman, "you did not preach the cross." The evangelist thoroughly concurred and made a resolution that night that he would never preach again without specifically lifting up Christ and Him crucified. Let us never forget the words of the apostle: "For the preaching of the cross is to them that perish, foolishness; but unto us which are saved, it is the power of God" (1 Cor. 1:18).

So we have seen that proclamation is related to the message of the preacher.

But in the second place, I want you to observe that:

Proclamation Is Related to the Manner of the Preacher

We need systematic teaching in order that the people of God might grow and relate their faith to everyday life. After Barnabas had established the church at Antioch, he brought the apostle Paul there for a whole year to teach and edify. It could be argued that the greatest need of our day is for that kind of teaching.

"And I was with you in weakness, and in fear, and in much trembling. And my speech and my preaching was not with enticing words of man's wisdom, but in demonstration of the Spirit and of power" (vv. 3–4).

In His inscrutable wisdom, God has chosen people like you and me to be preachers of the gospel. The awesomeness of this calling is well-nigh overwhelming when we realize that "God had only one Son and He made Him a preacher."[7] It follows, therefore, that the nearer we conform to the character of our Lord, the more effective we shall be as preachers. Paul underscores this in the text before us when he describes what should be the manner of the preacher. Three characteristics suggest themselves:

The Humility of Christ

"And I was with you in weakness, and in fear, and in much trembling" (v. 3). Commentators are not all agreed as to what Paul means by these words. Some suggest that the apostle was referring here to physical weakness (see 2 Cor. 12:7), and particularly to his "bodily presence" and "contemptible speech" (2 Cor. 10:10). Others maintain that this great preacher was acutely conscious of the shocking wickedness and the bitter antagonism that awaited him in Corinth. But over and above this was surely the self-distrust which his sensitive spirit experienced as he contemplated the exalted mission of preaching the cross. William Barclay renders it as "the trembling anxiety to perform a duty."[8]

This sense of helplessness in the work of God is the evidence of true humility. To quote Barclay again: "It is not the man who approaches a great task without a tremor who does it really well. The actor who is really great is the actor who is wrought up before the performance; the preacher who is really effective is the preacher whose heart beats faster while he waits to speak. The man who has no fear, no hesitancy, no nervousness, no tension, in any task, may give an efficient and competent performance; but it is the man who has this trembling anxiety, who has that intensity which is the essence of real greatness, *who can produce an effect which artistry alone can never achieve.*"[9]

In this connection it is well to remember Paul's words in his second letter to the Corinthians where he says, "Most gladly therefore will I rather glory in my infirmities, that the power of Christ may rest upon me" (12:9). Paul had long discovered that only when he was weak could he be strong.

And so it is today. The power of the Spirit can only rest upon those who know the humility of Christ. It is the broken life that God blesses, and it is the empty vessel that God fills. So Jesus says to you and me, "Learn of me; for I am meek and lowly in heart" (Matt. 11:29).

The Simplicity of Christ

"And my speech and my preaching was not with enticing words of man's wisdom" (v. 4).

Already Paul has said in the opening verses of this section: "And I, brethren, when I came to you, came not with excellency of speech or of wisdom, declaring unto you the testimony of God" (v. 1). The reference here, of course, is to what was known as "the Corinthian words." The philosophers and orators of Corinth were known for their Corinthian words of human eloquence and brilliant rhetoric. They were masters of "crowd psychology," as we would call it today. But such "speechifying" lacked the quality of real instruction or authoritative power.

The Bible teaches—and experience has proved—that one of the secrets of effectiveness in preaching is simplicity. This simplicity, of course, characterized our Savior's utterances. Read through His sermons and stories and you will be impressed all over again by the sheer simplicity and directness of His language. No wonder Paul exhorts the Corinthians to beware lest the devil, through his subtlety, should corrupt their minds from the simplicity that is in Christ (2 Cor. 11:3).

Today, our danger is that of preaching over the heads of people. The philosopher has a jargon of his own, and the physical scientist has his; and, alas, the preacher has his own brand, as well. If God is to own the message, then it has to be delivered in language understood by the people and in words dictated by the Spirit. This is implicit in that statement of the apostle where he says, "These things we also speak, not in words which man's wisdom teaches but which the Holy Spirit teaches" (v. 13 NKJV).

The Authority of Christ

"My speech and my preaching was . . . in demonstration of the Spirit and of power" (v. 4). This particular word rendered "demonstration" is used only here in the New Testament. Literally, it signifies "a showing forth" and has the force of *that which carries conviction through the power of the Holy Spirit*. What a definition of the authority of Christ!

When the Lord Jesus Christ preached in the days of His flesh, we read that "the people were astonished at his doctrine: for he taught them as one having authority, and not as the scribes" (Matt. 7:28–29). He spoke not only as One who imparted truth, but as One who was the living demonstration and embodiment of truth. This is why preaching has been defined as "truth through personality."[10] And Dr. H. H. Farmer defines preaching in the words of John's majestic prologue, "The Word became flesh."

Only when a man wields "the sword of the Spirit, which is the word of God" (Eph. 6:17), is proclamation authoritative. When Jesus spoke, people had to make a decision. They either believed on Him or picked up stones to stone Him. He never neutralized either individuals or congregations. His utterances were both incisive and decisive; and this is the evidence of the authority of heaven.

Now the secret of this humility, simplicity, and authority is found in the words of our Savior who said, "Ye shall receive power, after that the Holy Spirit is come upon you" (Acts 1:8). This is the anointing of the Spirit. It is more than the filling, even though it includes the filling. It is an anointing which gives, first of all, *the ability to appreciate the Word of God*. John says, "Ye have an unction from the Holy One, and ye know all things . . . and ye need not that any man teach you" (1 John 2:20, 27). And secondly, it is an anointing which gives *the authority to communicate the Word of God*. This is undoubtedly Paul's thought in 2 Corinthians 1, where he reminds his readers that his preaching of Christ was not sometimes "yea" and other times "nay," but rather an unwavering *yea,* since God had established him in Christ and also anointed him (vv. 20–21).

So we have seen that the manner of the preacher has a lot to do with either the evidence of power or the absence of it. Oh, to know the mighty filling and anointing of the Spirit which bring the humility, simplicity, and authority of apostolic preaching!

In the third and last place, I want to show that:

Proclamation Is Related to the Motive of the Preacher

"That your faith should not stand in the wisdom of men, but in the power of God" (v. 5).

Richard Roberts, in his book, *The Preacher as Man of Letters,* says: "It is our calling to persuade and . . . to convince. That is not preaching which is not preaching for a verdict."[11]

With the proclamation there must be the invitation. If the proclamation is the declaration of that which God has done and is doing in Christ and His cross, then the invitation is the call to men and women to respond to this Good News. If this is not our motive, then our preaching will be

129

powerless and fruitless. God never releases His power for personal aggrandizement or carnal objectives; on the contrary, He only sends His Holy Spirit to seal unto the day of redemption that which fulfills His redemptive purposes. Therefore, the motive of the preacher must be to lead men and women into an experience of a sound, saving, and steadfast faith in Christ. Let us take a few moments to amplify this further. No preacher of the gospel fulfills what God has designed unless men and women come to repose their faith in the power of God, which is Jesus Christ and Him crucified. This commitment to Christ is what Paul describes as:

A Sound Faith

"That your *faith* should not stand in the wisdom of men" (v. 5).

In the preceding verses of this epistle, Paul has demolished the notion that faith can be sound when reposed in the wisdom of men. In the language of the apostle James, such wisdom is "earthly, sensual, [and] devilish" (James 3:15). On the other hand, to be sound, faith must be exercised in the Savior Himself without dependence upon this human wisdom. Paul develops this point when he writes later concerning the death and resurrection of the Lord Jesus. He declares, "If Christ be not raised, your faith is vain; ye are yet in your sins" (1 Cor. 15:17). If Christ were not alive from the dead, then sin was not put away, the gospel was not true, the Christians had believed a lie, the apostles were false witnesses, and the loved ones who had fallen asleep were lost forever.

So to be sound in the faith, men and women must believe in the Son of God who literally and physically rose from the dead. All other tenets of the evangelical faith are both included and implied in the great doctrine of the death and resurrection of Jesus Christ.

But with a sound faith there must be:

A Saving Faith

"That your faith should not stand in the wisdom of men, but *in the power of God*" (v. 5).

Paul has already interpreted to us the meaning of the power of God in the previous chapter. You remember how he says that "the preaching of the cross is to them that perish, foolishness; but unto us which are *saved,* it is the power of God" (1 Cor. 1:18). Saving faith, to Paul, was a faith which had and was effecting a mighty transformation in the believing soul. It meant knowing the Lord Jesus Christ as Savior and Master, in every sense of the word.

So our motive, as preachers, is to bring our listeners to a sound, saving, and then

A Steadfast Faith

"That your faith should not *stand* in the wisdom of men, but in the power of God" (v. 5).

It has been well said that "what depends upon a clever argument is at the mercy of a more clever argument." This is not so, however, when faith is centered in the unchanging Son of God. This is what Paul means by a faith which "stands . . . in the power of God." The word conveys the idea of "steadfastness." Twice over in this epistle he exhorts the believers to be steadfast in the faith. The first mention follows the glorious treatment of the unalterable facts of the death and resurrection of our Lord and Savior Jesus Christ in chapter 15. Having declared the Son of God as the triumphant One, he says, "Be ye steadfast, unmovable, always abounding in the work of the Lord, forasmuch as ye know that your labor is not in vain in the Lord" (15:58). The second occurrence coincides with the conclusion of the epistle, where the apostle expresses his parting word to the believers at Corinth in these terms: "Watch ye, stand fast in the faith, quit you like men, be strong" (16:13).

Here, then, we have the supreme motive of the preacher: that the faith of his hearers should not stand in the wisdom of men, but in the power of God.

So we see that to be pure in our motives is to be powerful in our preaching. When the purpose of God is fulfilled, the Spirit of God confirms the Word "with signs following."

It is not without significance that Paul describes the object of preaching in terms of settling men and women "in the power of God." It follows, therefore, that only when this "power" is manifest is declaration authentic and effective.

Thus we have seen what we mean by evangelistic proclamation. No greater task has ever been entrusted to the sons of men. And in these days of what Dr. J. I. Packer calls "The Lost Word"[12] we need to recapture not only the glory of preaching, but also the power of preaching. As R. H. Fuller has put it, "In preaching God speaks, God acts, God produces faith . . . God builds up the Church."[13] And I might add, through preaching God revives the church.

John Stott says: "I believe that the teaching of the Word of God is the clue to the renewal of the church." And then he adds, "I agree with Martyn Lloyd-Jones in his book *Preaching and Preachers* that 'that most decadent periods in church history have always been those periods when preaching has declined.'" Stott maintains that the level of the church's teaching and preaching ministry, at the present time, is abysmal, and that as evangelicals who hold a high doctrine of Scripture, we ought to be the most conscientious in our exposition of the Word.[14]

Bishop Carl J. Sanders of Alabama, writing on the need to improve the quality and priority of preaching, says: "In the multiple tasks of a pastor, his identity as a 'preacher' may be lost; the quality of his preaching may decline as he fills other functions and neglects the disciplines required for effectual preaching; and confidence in the superior efficacy of preaching may fade as other ministries appear to be more redemptive. . . . History proves, however, that the church can exist without buildings, without liturgies, without choirs, without Sunday Schools, without professional clergymen, without creeds, without even women's societies. But the church cannot possibly exist without preaching the Word. Preaching has power like nothing else the church has or does. Moreover, preaching reaches more people than anything else the preacher can do, whether it is teaching, visiting, administering or counseling. . . . The time has come to restore preaching to its rightful place, its primary position in the work of the ministry. In preaching there is power! The power of the Spirit is the power of the Word. As the Word is proclaimed, the Spirit is busy working in the mind and heart of the hearer. Rise up, O man of God, and preach!"[15]

NOTES

1. F. D. Coggan, *The Ministry of the Word* (London: The Canterbury Press, 1945), p. 11.
2. *The Unity of the New Testament*, p. 22. Quoted in *The Ministry of the Word*, p. 66.
3. Coggan, pp. 62–63.
4. *The Nature and Purpose of the Gospels*, p. 80. Quoted in *The Ministry of the Word*, p. 33.
5. *The Ministry of the Word*, p. 61.
6. Charles John Ellicott, ed., *Elliott's Commentary on the Whole Bible*, vol. vii (Grand Rapids: Zondervan Publishing House, 1959), p. 292.

7. Thomas Goodwin. Quoted in *The Ministry of the Word*, p. 19.
8. William Barclay, *The Letters to the Corinthians*, 2nd ed. The Daily Study Bible Series (Philadelphia: The Westminster Press, 1956), p. 27.
9. Ibid.
10. Phillips Brooks, *Lectures on Preaching* (Grand Rapids: Zondervan Publishing House), p. 7.
11. p. 47. Quoted in *The Ministry of the Word*, p. 19.
12. *God Hath Spoken* (London: Hodder & Stoughton, 1965), p. 9.
13. *Theology*, vol. xlvii, p. 271. Quoted in *The Ministry of the Word*, p. 13.
14. John Capon, "We Must Begin with the Glory of God," *Crusade*, May 1974, p. 36.
15. *The United Methodist Reporter*, January 11, 1974, p. 2.
Scripture quotations in this article are from the KING JAMES VERSION of the Bible.

Part 3:
Preaching: God's Message

The Cost of Being a Disciple

GERALD B. GRIFFITHS

What is a disciple?" I asked myself. As I read the words of Jesus, I realized there are two very different kinds of disciples in this world: those who follow Jesus and those who follow a human leader, for instance, Karl Marx.

Marx was a leader in his day, but now his disciples follow him only so far. Mikhail Gorbachev, an avowed disciple of Marx, does not agree with everything Marx said. Nor does Mrs. Gorbachev. Certainly not Mrs. Gorbachev. She actually tells Russian women to dress as they like; she wants to put the Vogue pattern book beside Marx's *Das Kapital*—an idea which would have made Marx's hair stand on end! But the Gorbachevs are only being sensible. Marx was, after all, only a child of his age. His teaching is clearly out of step with the economic realities of today. All human leaders are like Karl Marx—wrong at some point—and their disciples, if they have any sense, follow them so far and no further. But not so the disciples of Jesus!

The Disciples of Jesus Are Different

Jesus is never wrong or out of date. He is not like Marx or Plato or a rabbi—a mere leader of thought. Jesus is the Son of God. And His first disciples recognized Him as the Son of God and the Lord of the universe. They called Him "Lord" and He accepted the title. "You call Me 'Teacher' and 'Lord'" He said, "and rightly so, for that is what I am" (John 13:13).[1]

The first disciples were excited when they discovered who Jesus really was. Andrew hurried back to his brother Simon and exclaimed, "We have found the Messiah!" (John 1:41). Nathanael burst out, "Rabbi, You are the Son of God! You are the King of Israel!" (John 1:49). Simon Peter burst out too: "You are the Christ, the Son of the living God!" (Matt. 16:16). Thomas the doubter fell on his knees when he saw the risen Lord that first Sunday night after Easter. He worshipped Him and cried out,

137

"My Lord and my God!" (John 20:28). And when Saul of Tarsus met the exalted Christ on the way to Damascus, he surrendered to Him immediately: "What shall I do, Lord?" (Acts 22:10).

The first disciples followed Jesus because they had discovered who He really was: the Son of God, the Sovereign Lord of the universe. And when they discovered who Jesus was, they discovered who they were: His *slaves*. If Jesus was their teacher, they were His students. If Jesus was their leader, they were His followers. If Jesus was their Lord, they were His slaves.

The newly converted Saul of Tarsus realized this. That is why he immediately asked, "Lord, what do you want me to do?" as if to say, "Command me! I am your slave." All through his Christian life Paul called himself "a slave of Jesus Christ." And he was right. For this is what Jesus told His disciples again and again: "If I am your Lord, you are my slaves."[2]

If Jesus Is Lord, We Are His Slaves

But what does it mean to be a slave of Jesus Christ? What did it mean to be a slave in the days of Jesus? It meant being totally submissive to one's master and owner. In ancient Rome, a slave belonged to his owner absolutely, like a chair or a table, or a sheep or a goat. A slave had no legal rights; his life was controlled completely by his owner.

And this is how we belong to Jesus Christ if we are His disciples. He owns us completely, by right of creation and by right of purchase (John 1:10; 1 Peter 1:18). "You are not your own; you were bought at a price"—the infinite price of the blood of God's Son (1 Cor. 6:19–20).

So this is what we must do to become a disciple of Jesus Christ: we must surrender ourselves absolutely to Him; we must become His slaves. But the crowds going with Jesus to Jerusalem did not understand this. On the contrary, they thought of Jesus as *their* slave.

To them Jesus was a tool, a miracle-worker to put their country straight, a political messiah to overthrow the Romans and make Israel independent and prosperous.

Are we like these crowds? Do we think of Jesus as our slave, as our tool? When we are short of money, do we turn to Jesus just to get instant cash? When we have enough money but want more, do we turn to Jesus because we imagine him to be the positive thinker par excellence who guarantees His clients health and wealth unlimited? When we have family problems, do we call in Jesus as if He were the local plumber who will mend the burst pipe in our marriage and then politely leave us alone to do our own thing? When we have emotional problems, do we expect Jesus to be a psychologist who will soothe our hurt egos—and leave our cruel self free to strike again? How do we think of Jesus? As an obliging Mr. Fix-it? If so, we are mistaken.

Jesus is Lord! The Son of God! The Savior who has bought us and freed us from our sins by His own blood. And we owe him nothing less than our total allegiance.

But many in the crowds going with Him to Jerusalem had no intention of giving Jesus their total allegiance. Oh, no! And that is why our Lord held up a restraining hand and spelled out plainly to the crowds—and to us—what it costs to be His disciple.

What does it cost to be a disciple?

The Cost

We Must Put Christ First Before Our Own Family:

If anyone comes to me and does not hate [does not put in the second place] his father and mother, his wife and children, his brothers and sisters . . . he cannot be my disciple (Luke 14:26).

We must love our families. Of course! Love them dearly. But we must love the Lord first of all.

We Must Put Christ First Even Before Our Own Life:

If anyone comes to me and does not hate [does not put in the second place] . . . even his own life, he cannot be my disciple (Luke 14:26).

Indeed, we must be *willing to die* for Christ's sake, and to die the most shameful and painful death, death by crucifixion:

Anyone who does not carry his cross and follow me cannot be my disciple (Luke 14:27).

Millions of Christians have chosen to die rather than deny their Lord. James the brother of John was beheaded. So was Paul. Stephen was 139 stoned to death. In first-century Rome, believers were covered with pitch and burned alive, and many were thrown to the lions. In the last nineteen hundred years millions of Christians have died a martyr's death. Some of their sufferings are recorded in *Fox's Book of Martyrs* and in James and Marty Hefley's *By Their Blood*,[3] a sobering saga of twentieth-century martyrs. More Christians have died for their faith in this century than in all the other centuries put together. To this day Christians are martyred in shocking numbers: an average of three hundred thirty thousand a year, according to researcher David Barrett.

Of course, not every disciple dies a martyr's death. But there is a death that every Christian must die: a death to our sinful self. You know what I am talking about if you are a Christian.

When we first came to Christ we had to die to our sinful self. We had to say a decisive no to our old nature; we had to crucify it, with its passions and desires (Gal. 5:24). But this was not the end of our dying to self. It was only the beginning!

We have to die every day—a thousand times, if need be. Every day we live on earth we must resist the clamors of our old nature. Resist! Resist! Resist! This is what the Bible says: "Put to death . . . whatever belongs to your earthly nature: sexual immorality, impurity, lust, evil desires and greed" (Col. 3:5).

Christ's invitation to us has two sides to it. One side says "Come and *dine*"; the other says "Come and *die*." "When Christ calls a man," says Dietrich Bonhoeffer, "he bids him come and die."[4]

The call to die is an essential part of the gospel. "Come and die to your pride and self-will," the Lord says to us, "Come and die to your greed and passion, to your resentment and anger, to your love of success and praise, to your coldness toward God and your neighbor. Come and die to sin that you may live to righteousness" (see 1 Peter 2:24). Before we can dine at the King's banqueting table, we must die to self (see Rom. 8:13).

"Total surrender is what I demand," says the Lord Jesus, "the total submission of a slave to his master. Before you enlist as my disciples, make sure you have counted the cost and you are ready to pay the price of total surrender."

Count the Cost First

Wise people count the cost first. They do not rush into things they cannot finish.

Suppose one of you wants to build a tower. Will he not first sit down and estimate the cost to see if he has enough money to complete it? For if he lays the foundation and is not able to finish it, everyone who sees it will ridicule him, saying, "This fellow began to build and was not able to finish" (Luke 14:28–30).

No farmer, says Jesus, would dream of starting a project like building a tower in his vineyard without first making sure he could finish it. If he did not finish it, he would become the laughingstock of the village, and for years to come his tower would be a standing joke.

Or suppose a king is about to go to war against another king. Will he not first sit down and consider whether he is able with ten thousand men to oppose the one coming against him with twenty thousand? If he is not able, he will send a delegation while the other is still a long way off and will ask for terms of peace (Luke 14:31–32).

No king would dream of plunging into a battle against an army twice the size of his own. He would count the cost first, and if he saw he could not win, he would not start a fight.

"In the same way," our Lord says to the crowds, "do not start to follow me unless you are prepared to face all the consequences, unless you are ready to pay the price." And He repeats what the price is: surrender to Him. . . . "any of you who does not give up everything he has cannot be my disciple" (Luke 14:33).

Without total surrender no one can become Jesus' disciple. Does this mean that without this total surrender no one can become a *Christian?*

Do We Have to Surrender All to Become a Christian?

Some answer, "No, we can be Christians without surrendering all to Jesus." And they give their reason for saying we can be Christians on easier terms. It is simply that: *a person can be a Christian without becoming a disciple.* A disciple, they say, is a step above an ordinary Christian; a disciple is a growing Christian, a dedicated Christian, a superior brand of Christian.

No, he isn't! In the New Testament a disciple and a Christian are one and the same. In the beginning all followers of Jesus were called disciples. Then later on, in Syria, in the city of Antioch, they were called Christians, as Luke tells us in Acts 11:26: "The disciples were first called Christians in Antioch." So if Jesus says we must leave all in order to become His disciple, it follows that we must leave all in order to become a Christian.

We cannot dodge our Lord's demand for full surrender by saying "Well, only disciples have to give up everything and I don't want to be a disciple; all I want to be is an ordinary, run-of-the-mill Christian. Therefore I can pick and choose what I give up, what I surrender to Christ. Granted, if I were going on to be a disciple, that would be another story; then I'd have to take the high road. But seeing I'm only going to be a plain Christian, I can take the low road."

Heresy! The Lord does not give us the option of taking the high road or the low road. He offers us one road only: the narrow road that leads to life (see Matt. 7:14).

Yes

To become a Christian we must own Jesus Christ as Lord (Rom. 10:9) and ourselves as His slaves (Rom. 6:17–22). At the time of our conversion, we must declare our intent to trust and obey Him, whatever the cost.

To be sure, at the time of our conversion we may not understand all the implications of entrusting ourselves completely to Christ. I certainly didn't! But we must understand the basic fact that we are entrusting ourselves to Christ and promising to follow Him all the way.

In practice, what does this mean? An Asian Christian gets down to brass tacks:

> One who trusts in Christ alone [will] completely give up his idols, horoscopes and other such practices of his old life that go against Christ's Lordship. When a true believer is made aware of any area of his life that is not yielded to Christ, he will yield it. When he is made aware of a Christian principle to be followed, he will follow it whatever the cost.
>
> So when a new believer finds out that a follower of Christ should love his enemies, he will do so, even though that seems sheer folly in today's society.
>
> When he finds out that a follower of Christ cannot pay a bribe, he will stop paying bribes and pay dearly for it as far as his success in society is concerned. When he finds out that a follower of Christ treats both high and low caste people, both rich and poor people as equals, he will do so, however hard that may be for him.[5]

In the words of the Lord Jesus, as we have seen, entrusting ourselves to Him means putting Him first in our lives, first before our nearest and dearest, first before our most prized possessions and prospects, first before life itself. It means being willing to die to all things in order that Christ may be honored and served. It means making Jesus Christ Lord of all we are and have and hope to be. In the gospel, Christ calls us into a new relationship with Him, where He is our Lord and we are His willing slaves, who yield to Him even the thing we cherish most—our right to ourselves.

Now let's go back to the picture of Jesus with His hand up to stop would-be disciples, bandwagon jumpers.

Does this picture apply to any of us? Is He saying stop to you now? What do you think of Jesus? Why do you want to come to Him? Is He holding up His hand now to tell you, "No, my friend, you are not ready to come to Me yet"?

If so, you will be ready when you see what comes immediately before this in Luke 14: the picture of Jesus the Great Welcomer.

Jesus the Great Welcomer

How we love this picture! Jesus stands before us with His arms outstretched to welcome all who are weary and weighed down with failure and sorrow and sin and shame, to welcome all who long for God's forgiveness and freedom. See Him now! His arms are open wide to welcome you, to welcome all who have discovered who He is: the Son of God, the crucified Savior, the risen Lord.

When you come to Him, what will He give you? What no man can give you: pardon and peace, a new life and a new name. He will make you a child of God, an inheritor of the kingdom, a member of His body in this world. He will come to live in you and love through you. He will open wide His arms, take you in, and make you what you never dreamed you could be.

And how then shall we say thank you? With our partial allegiance? That would be sacrilege!

The Only Right Response

How shall we say thank you? With everything we possess! With all we have and are! How else? C. T. Studd was right: "If Jesus Christ be God 143 and died for me, then no sacrifice can be too great for me to make for Him."

Jesus Christ must have all of me, and all of you. Will you join me now in the only response a redeemed sinner can make to his Lord and Savior:

> All for Jesus! All for Jesus!
> All my being's ransomed powers;
> All my thoughts and words and doings,
> All my days and all my hours.[6]

All for Jesus!

NOTES

1. "For all the formal similarities, there is no inner relation between the *talmid* [disciple] of the rabbis and the *mathetes* [disciple] of Jesus. Jesus is *kyrios* [Lord], not rabbi." K. H. Rengstorf, "Disciple *mathetes*," in *The Theological Dictionary of the New Testament*, eds. Kittel and Friedrich (Grand Rapids: William B. Eerdmans, 1985), pp. 560–6.
2. "Jesus requires that his disciples leave all things for his sake alone (Matt. 10:37ff). In so doing, they are not merely to believe in him; they are to obey him as *douloi* [slaves] obey their *kyrios* [master, Lord]." Ibid.
3. James and Marty Hefley, *By Their Blood* (Milford, Mich.: Mott Media, 1979).
4. Dietrich Bonhoeffer, *The Cost of Discipleship* (London: SCM Press, 1962), p. 7.
5. Ajith Fernando, *The Christian's Attitude Toward World Religions* (Wheaton, Ill.: Tyndale House Publishers, 1987).
6. Mary D. James, "All for Jesus! All for Jesus!", 1889, *Hymns for the Living Church* (Carol Stream, Ill.: Hope Publishing Co., 1980).

Scripture quotations in this article are from the NEW INTERNATIONAL VERSION of the Bible. Copyright © 1978 by New York International Bible Society.

The Quality of Commitment

W. IAN THOMAS

But Jesus did not commit himself unto them, because he knew all men (John 2:24).

All that glitters is not gold," and in the light of all that we are about to consider, it may well be profitable for us to make a sober reevaluation of those standards of commitment which are prevalent today, and which pass muster for Christian dedication.

All too often quantity takes precedence over quality, and in this highly competitive age these outward appearances of "success" which are calculated to enhance the reputation of the professional preacher, or the prestige of those who have promoted him, are of greater importance than the abiding consequences of his ministry.

In an unholy ambition to get results the end too often justifies the means, with the result that the means are certainly not always beyond suspicion, and the results, to say the least, extremely dubious!

In this unhappy situation both the pulpit and the pew carry their share of the blame, though I suspect that it started in the pulpit! There are those who have insisted that to be valid, every spiritual transaction between the believer and his Lord must be matched by some outward physical act, and that apart from the accompanying act, no worth can be attached to the inward spiritual transaction.

Inevitably on the basis of this unfounded supposition, the work of the Holy Spirit in any given meeting through the ministry of the preacher, will be directly represented by the physical response of the congregation to some form of public appeal, "invitation" or so-called "altar call"—a term which is singularly inappropriate in view of the fact that the Lord Jesus Christ has "offered one sacrifice for sins forever" (Heb. 10:12), and there is no place today for another sacrifice or for another altar in the 145

Church of the redeemed—the altar has given place to a throne for the exalted Lamb!

The terrible dangers inherent in such a fallacy, however, are patently obvious! The ambitious preacher, eager to climb the ladder of evangelical fame, and not altogether unmoved by the plight of the lost and the needs of the saints, will be subject to a temptation so strong, that for more than one it has proved to be irresistible, that of being heavily preoccupied with devising ways and means of ensuring that a large enough public "response" on the part of the congregation will adequately demonstrate the effectiveness of his preaching, vindicate his reputation, sufficiently reward the confidence of his sponsors and suitably impress the crowd.

The preacher, of course, will not allow himself to be aware of the underlying motives which prompt the use of his clever techniques, being careful to persuade himself that they stem only from what he would describe as genuine "passion for souls," but the sorry spectacle is exposed for what it is by the apparent indifference on the part of the preacher to the tragic aftermath of his endeavors, once "the show is over"!

It is little wonder that the "pulpit," having drilled the "pew" into submission, now finds itself the victim of its own ill-conceived imposition, for the community which has been taught to accept outward, physical response to some public "invitation" as the criterion of spiritual success on the part of the preacher, invariably demands this tangible evidence of success on every occasion in which he engages in his ministry.

Thus the pastor of a small church, trapped in the grip of this vicious circle, may succeed over a period of time in bringing the whole of his congregation "out to the front"—to stand at the communion rail in response to his many appeals—but having had all his people out once, it will be incumbent upon him to get them out all over again, and again, and yet *again* if his fervor and his zeal are not to be called into question by his church officers, and his pastorate, maybe, become vacant!

The pastor has no option under such circumstances, but to whittle down the commitment he demands until its whole value and meaning has been lost, for it can never be final, otherwise he would preach himself out of business! Instead of being faced with complete capitulation to the Lord Jesus Christ, and final, irrevocable abandonment to all *His* will, the believer is presented again and again with "baby" issues, all of which should be comprehended in the greater, basic issue of true discipleship!

It is much easier to confront a person with his *sins* than it is to confront

him with his "sin," for "sin" is an attitude which affects a man's fundamental relationship to God; it has to do with what a man is; whereas
"sins" have to do with what a man *does*. We all have a happy knack of
being able to detach what we do from what we are! We are all highly
skilled in the art of self-justification and are able to produce innumerable
reasons as to why what we did was excusable—even if it was wrong! We
can even feel heroic, and almost virtuous, in accepting the blame for that
which so obviously *(to us)* was only the *natural,* almost inevitable reaction to enticing, compelling or provocative circumstances or people! For
this reason a man can admit and be sorry for what he has done, without
admitting that what he has done is a result of what he is.

On this basis a person may be called upon a hundred times to face the
lesser issues of what he has done, without once being confronted with the
greater issue of what he is—indeed the "comfort" to be found in confession, bringing freedom from fear and relief to a bad conscience will elimi-
nate for him the need for any basic change in his fundamental relationship
to God. This kind of confession falls hopelessly short of real repentance,
and remains unmatched by any change of purpose. Moses reduced his
people to tears again and again, but it left them in the wilderness! They
still had no heart for Canaan! There was no lack of response to Moses'
preaching, but they would not do business with God! "And they said unto
Moses, Speak thou with us, and we will hear: but let not God speak with
us, lest we die" (Ex. 20:19).

They wanted second-hand religion! They wanted neither godlessness
nor godliness—they did not know how to live, and were afraid to die!
Commitment to them was on the installment system, and Moses was their
broker!

Secondhand religion may keep a preacher in business, and make him
indispensible to his congregation, but it cannot produce discipleship;
there will be no spontaneity of action, nor any other evidence of that divine initiative in man which springs only from man's total availability to
God.

True commitment to the Lord Jesus Christ gives Him the "right of
way," and releases His life through you in all the freshness and power of
divine action, so that according to His gracious promise, out of your in-
nermost being "springs and rivers of living water may flow continuously"
(John 7:38, *Amplified New Testament*)—and you do not have to push a
river! It cuts its own channel, and cleanses as it flows!

147

In drawing attention to those glaring abuses which have done so much to discredit modern evangelism and convention ministry, I do not suggest for one moment, that there is not a legitimate place for the public confession of faith in Christ, nor would I insist that true commitment to Christ may never be accompanied by an outward witness to the fact. That would be to throw away the baby with the bath-water, for without a doubt, there are many who have been greatly helped in their *decision* for Christ, or in their commitment *to* Christ by a wise, gracious invitation to *act,* rather than further to delay in yielding obedience to the Truth.

My plea is simply for *reality* on God's terms of reference! It is for this reason also, that no matter how intensely I may dislike the shallowness and showmanship of many in their abuse of the holy act of preaching, by the use of doubtful "response techniques," I cannot on the other hand, endorse in any way the empty accusation made by the champions of hollow, ritualistic formalism, that all activity outside the established "practice of religion" within the "respectable church systems" is of necessity all "mere ignorant emotionalism." That is sheer nonsense!

If there remains much to be desired in the quality of commitment prevalent today in evangelical circles, and in the worldwide evangelistic outreach of that great body of born-again believers which is the true Church of Jesus Christ, in all denominations—even more to be deplored are those wholesale opportunities for practicing hypocrisy provided by those formal, public acts of commitment to Christ which are common to so many of the denominations and which in the vast majority of cases are totally devoid of any spiritual content, serving only to satisfy the traditional "niceties" of religious observance in an otherwise godless society!

Whether it be by baptism as an infant or as an adult, by "sprinkling" or by "immersion," whether it be by confirmation in the early "teens," or by any other public act of dedication and acceptance into full church membership, there must be very few in the "Christianized" countries of the Western World who have not in one way or another, "committed themselves to Christ." Yet by what strange twist of the mind or willful stretch of the imagination, any ecclesiastical hierarchy of any given church system can credit this performance with any real spiritual validity, when in many cases over 90 percent of the population of these countries never darken a church door to worship God, is beyond all intelligent explanation! The Lord Jesus Christ is neither accepted as Savior nor honored and obeyed as Lord, yet the rubber stamp of church approval has been granted, and is considered by the overwhelming majority to be an altogether adequate discharge of their responsibility toward God, and a formidable defense against the unwelcome attentions of those who would insist upon a reality of spiritual experience, which has neither been explained, demanded nor expected by their "church"!

If church attendance in the United States, representing something like 40 percent of the population, far and away exceeds that of any other Protestant country at this time, it should be a matter of genuine thankfulness to God—yet there are few countries in the world where there are so many crimes of violence, so much juvenile delinquency, so much drug addiction and so many alcoholics, and where there is such widespread graft and corruption in government and commerce. Are only *those* responsible for this sorry record who have never conformed to the requirements of the church, in some outward, formal act of dedication?

Why should international world Communism with its fanatical convictions, its thorough indoctrination and utter dedication, be afraid of this flabby monster called "the church," with its countless millions of nominal adherents who know neither conviction nor concern—who are colorless, spiritual nonentities, knowing neither what they believe, nor believing what they know! They are utterly without any sense of mission, and governed by and large by men who are themselves riddled through and through with infidelity, boastful of their own wanton repudiation of all the essential ingredients of the faith they profess to proclaim! A Christendom whose worst enemies are within its own ranks!

The Word of God to the Jews in Paul's day might well be the Word of God to Christendom today:

> For, as it is written, The name of God is magnified and blasphemed among the Gentiles because of you! The words to this effect are from [your own] Scriptures . . . For he is not a [real] Jew who is only one outwardly and publicly, nor is [true] circumcision something external or physical. But he is a Jew who is one inwardly, and true circumcision is of the heart, a spiritual and not a literal [matter]. His praise is not from men but from God (Rom. 2:24, 28, 29, *Amplified New Testament*).

It was into just such a situation that the Lord Jesus Christ entered, as at the Feast of the Passover He received such a tumultuous welcome in Jerusalem. "Hosanna to the Son of David!" they cried. "Blessed be he that cometh in the name of the Lord: Hosanna in the highest" (Matt. 21:9). 149

No doubt the disciples were flushed with excitement and highly delighted that their Master should receive such a tremendous ovation—yet maybe there were some among them who had their misgivings! If only He could be prevailed upon not to say the wrong thing! If only they could persuade Him just this once, not to do anything which would spoil it all!

But He did it again!

What a heartbreak Christ would be today to some well-meaning promotional "committee" or to some "business manager!" It seemed that He always did the wrong thing or said the wrong thing, just as He was on the crest of the wave, and at the height of His popularity! He never seemed to understand what was in His own best interests!

Amidst all this popular acclaim, the Lord Jesus Christ went straight to the temple and found:

> Those that sold oxen and sheep and doves, and the changers of money sitting: And when he had made a scourge of small cords, he drove them all out of the temple, and the sheep, and the oxen; and poured out the changers' money, and overthrew the tables; And said unto them that sold doves, Take these things hence; make not my Father's house a house of merchandise (John 2:14–16).

Had He been prepared to accept "religion" as He found it, and recognize the "status quo," no doubt the Lord Jesus Christ might well have found acceptance, even among the Pharisees; but He was a trouble maker! He dared to cleanse the temple!

Christ did not come to the "accepted," nor was He "looking for a 'job'" in contemporary religion! He came to cleanse the temple—and to do a bigger job than just to cleanse the temple in Jerusalem; He had come to cleanse the temples of men's hearts, that they might be fit again to be "an habitation of God through the Spirit" (Eph. 2:22).

Challenged to declare by what authority He presumed to disapprove, and by what authority He was prepared to translate His disapproval into action, the Lord Jesus Christ gave this answer: "Destroy this temple, and in three days I will raise it up. But this spake He of the temple of His body" (John 2:19, 21).

Christ's death and resurrection were to be His mandate, and commitment to Christ for anything less than to be cleansed from sin and inhabited by God misses the whole point of the cross! He will accept nothing less!

150

Now when he was in Jerusalem at the passover, in the feast day, many believed in his name, when they saw the miracles which he did. But Jesus did not commit himself unto them, because he knew all men, and needed not that any should testify of man: for he knew what was in man (John 2:23–25).

Although the crowd appeared to have committed themselves to Christ, the quality of their commitment was such that He was not prepared to commit Himself to them!

What is the quality of your commitment to Christ?

You may be accepted into membership by the "church," approved by your friends and entrusted with responsible office, but of what possible value can these things be, if your commitment to Christ is such that He is not willing to commit Himself to you? The value of your commitment to Christ will only be the measure of His commitment to you!

The Lord Jesus Christ is the Truth, and as in all other things "that pertain unto life and godliness" (2 Peter 1:3). He is the Truth about true commitment. He was committed to the Father for all that to which the Father was committed to the Son, and He was supremely confident that the Father who dwelt in Him was gloriously adequate for all that to which He was committed. We know also that His commitment to His Father was such that the Father was completely committed to His Son!

The Lord Jesus Christ refused to be committed to the parochial needs of His own day and generation; He was not committed to the political situation in Palestine, nor to the emancipation of the Jewish nation from the Roman yoke! He was not committed to the pressing social problems of His time, nor to one faction as opposed to another, any more than today He is committed to the West against the East, or to Republicans against the Democrats (as though either were less wicked than the other!). Christ was not even committed to the needs of a perishing world; He was neither unmindful nor unmoved by all these other issues, but as Perfect Man He was committed to His Father, and for that only which His Father was committed to in Him—exclusively!

Then said Jesus unto them, "When ye have lifted up the Son of man, then shall ye know that I am He, and that I do nothing of myself; but as my Father hath taught me, I speak these things. And He that sent me is with me: The Father hath not left me alone; for I do always those things that please Him" (John 8:28, 29).

The Lord Jesus Christ was fully aware from the beginning of that to which the Father was committed in Him, for He was "the Lamb slain from the foundation of the world" (Rev. 13:8). Breaking the bread which pictured His body so soon to be broken, and taking the wine as the symbol of His blood so soon to be shed, He could still look up into His Father's face and say "thank You!" He was completely committed, and there were no other issues then for Him to face!

The Lord Jesus Christ knew that before ever men like Wilberforce, Robert Moffat, and David Livingstone could be committed to Him for that to which He was to be committed in them—abolition of slavery and the restoration of human dignity in the quality of all men under God; before ever men like the Earl of Shaftesbury, Dr. Barnardo, and George Mueller could be committed to Him for that for which He was to be committed in them—to gather the ragged, half-starved orphans off the streets of Britain and restore hope to the unwanted; before He could attack the social evils and unschooled ignorance of a wanton nation through the persons of John Wesley and George Whitefield, during the great evangelical awakening of their century, or use Elizabeth Fry to bring about a reformation within an unpitying penal system which left a community of despair to languish, unloved and unmourned, in the vermin-ridden prisons of her land—He, the Son of God, had first to commit Himself to the Father for that to which the Father was committed in Him!

The basis of His commitment to the Father is the basis upon which the Lord Jesus Christ claims your commitment to Him; you are committed to Him for all that to which He is committed in you exclusively!

You are not committed to a church, nor to a denomination, nor to an organization; as a missionary you are not committed to a mission board nor even to a "field," and least of all are you committed to a "need"! You are committed to Christ, and for all that to which Christ is committed in you, and again I say—exclusively!

Thousands of earnest young Christians are challenged with the outworn slogan, "The need is the call!" and are then immediately presented with a dozen different needs, all representing a "call"! When the "invitation" is given, hundreds stand in their confusion, swept to their feet on a wave of sentiment, yet it has been determined on a strictly statistical basis that out of every one hundred who stand, not more than five will ever reach the mission field, and of those who do, almost 50 percent will return home to stay at home by the end of their first term overseas!

Moses mistook the need for the "call," and moved with compassion, went out to murder an Egyptian in defense of his brethren, becoming useless to God or man for forty years in the backside of the desert, herding a handful of sheep!

Abraham committed himself to the will of God, instead of to God whose will it was, and in his misguided zeal tried to do God's work man's way! He felt that it was up to him and to Sarai to help God out of His predicament, for Sarai was old and barren, so they had a committee meeting! After all, God had said that Abraham was to have a son, and if this was God's will—a son he must have, at any price!

It was a heavy price that Abraham paid as Hagar, Sarai's maid, was summoned and ill-begotten Ishmael was born. Ishmael was the by-product of a false commitment. Conceived in sincerity, Ishmael was the devil's *reasonable alternative to faith!*

When Isaac was born in God's perfect timing, fifteen years later, Ishmael mocked him—and he has been mocking him ever since! ". . . as then he that was born after the flesh persecuted him that was born after the Spirit, even so it is now" (Gal. 4:29); "O that Ishmael might live before Thee!" (Gen. 17:18) is still the cry of those who in our own day and generation have yet to learn that ". . . the son of the bondwoman shall not be heir with the son of the freewoman" (Gal. 4:30)—that there is *absolutely no substitute* so far as God is concerned, for God's work done God's way!

When God tested Abraham and told him to offer up Isaac for a burnt offering, He said, "Take now thy son, thine only son, whom thou lovest, and get thee into the land of Moriah" (Gen. 22:2). Abraham might have argued with God and said, "But I have two *sons!* What about Ishmael? Isaac is not my only son!" Then God would have replied, "So far as I am concerned, only Isaac is your son. I do not recognize Ishmael—he should never have been born!"

The Church of Jesus Christ today is plagued with Ishmael's clamoring to be recognized, but God will only honor Isaac, and Isaac's Greater Son! Nothing infuriates the "flesh" more than failure to be recognized, and preaching that exposes it for the wicked counterfeit it is must inevitably be the object of its venom and its wrath! "Too Subjective! Unrealistic! Otherworldly! Over-simplified! Mere passivity! Pantheistic mysticism!" These are some of the epithets with which "Ishmael" still mocks "Isaac"; with which the "flesh" resists the Spirit!

At God's command, Abraham took Isaac, bound him, laid him on the altar he had built, and took his knife to slay him, and with actions far more eloquent than words said to God by what he did, "You promised me Isaac! I did not see how You could do it, and in my unbelief and in my folly I produced my Ishmael; I committed myself to Your *will,* and thought I was more competent than God. Now You tell me to slay him, my *only* son Isaac in whom You have promised that all the families of the earth shall be blessed! O God, if I slay him, I do not see how You can do it—but now I am committed to *You*—exclusively, and to all that for which You are committed in me! If slay him I must, then slay him I will, even if You have to raise him from the dead!" (Heb. 11:17–19), and in so many words God said to Abraham, "Thank you, Abraham! That is all I wanted to know, now you can throw your knife away!"

> Lay not thine hand upon the lad, neither do thou anything unto him, for now I know that thou fearest God. By myself have I sworn, saith the Lord, for because thou hast done this thing, and hast not withheld thy son, thine only son. That in blessing I will bless thee, and in multiplying I will multiply thy seed as the stars of heaven, and as the sand which is upon the seashore; and thy seed shall possess the gate of his enemies; because thou hast obeyed my voice (Gen. 22:12, 16–18).

Abraham had learned the secret of true commitment, and became "the Friend of God" (James 2:23)! This is reality, and this is discipleship!

It is "godliness in action!" Presenting all that you are—*nothing,* to all that He is—*everything!* You are committed to the Lord Jesus Christ exclusively, for all that to which He is committed in you and you may be supremely confident that He who dwells in you, as the Father dwelt in Him, is gloriously adequate for all that to which He is committed!

Are you prepared for this to be the quality of your commitment to Christ? If so, then every lesser issue has been comprehended in the greater. It is now no longer necessary for me to ask you whether you are prepared to go to the mission field! It is now no longer necessary for me to ask you whether you are prepared to put your bank account at Christ's disposal, or your time, or your home, or face you with any other issue I could think of! You would say to me at once, "These issues now have all been settled—finally, once and for all! If Christ is committed in me to go to the mission field, I am already committed to Him for this! If He is committed in me to use the very last dollar I possess and every other dollar I shall ever earn, I am already committed to Him for that, and for everything and anything else to which He may be committed in me! There are no more issues for me to face, only His instructions to obey! I know too, that for all His will, I have all that He is! . . . and that is all I need to know!"

Indeed it is! . . . for you cannot have more!

And you need never have less!

NOTES

Scripture quotations in this article are from the KING JAMES VERSION of the Bible, and the AMPLIFIED BIBLE: Old Testament, copyright © 1962, 1964 by Zondervan Publishing House; and New Testament, copyright © 1958 by the Lockman Foundation.

This essay was originally published in *The Mystery of Godliness* by Major Ian Thomas (Grand Rapids, Mich.: Zondervan Publishing House, 1964).

The Making of a Man of God

ALAN REDPATH

Distance has separated Dr. and Mrs. Olford from my wife and me for the last several years, but we have known them since before their marriage and have been close in heart, often sharing in crusades, conferences, and conventions, rejoicing together in the goodness of God as we have seen lives transformed through the preaching of His Word. I remember Stephen Olford and I were both speaking at Columbia Bible College in South Carolina. We were preparing to leave to catch a plane when some students rushed up to us, notebooks and Bibles in hand, and one of them called out, "Gentlemen, please before you go: What is the key to Christian leadership?" Before I had time to think, Dr. Olford replied, "Bent knees, wet eyes, and a broken heart." That typifies the man himself and has been the secret of his most effective ministry through the years.

This is why I want to share some thoughts on the making of a man of God, as the man can make or mar the efficacy of the message he has to proclaim. Moses was right on target when he made his urgent plea to the Lord in Exodus 33:18, "I pray thee, show me thy glory." He did not ask for wisdom, eloquence, or a winsome personality, but to be swept up and bowled over by the glory of God. Moses was not content with the presence of the Lord, of which he was assured, but he wanted something more. No wonder we read in verse 11, "Thus the Lord used to speak to Moses face to face as a man speaks to his friend." The man of God must become the friend of God, and Jesus has said, "You are My friends if you do whatever I command you" (John 15:14).

So often in place of seeking God Himself we substitute work for worship, activity for communion, orthodoxy for obedience. So many of us, alas, go into the ministry without ever facing that important question, in complete contrast to the way the Lord Jesus Himself faced His coming ministry: "He went out to the mountain to pray, and continued all night in prayer to God" (Luke 6:12 NKJV). Let us then study what sort of person a *Christian leader* is to be.

He Must Be a Called Man

(See Luke 6:13.) It is important to consider very seriously just why an individual is prepared to be a Christian leader either at home or overseas rather than take up any other profession. Ask yourself, was it because friends suggested such a role, perhaps because you were good at speaking? Was it because you felt it would be a satisfying career, or because others you admire have succeeded in it? Or perhaps because you have failed in other things and thought Christian work would be easier? All these reasons are utterly inadequate. The only justification for being in the Lord's front rank is that you have been called by God. But, you may ask, "How do I know that?" The answer is not simple, but let me remind you that God was able to speak to Moses out of a bush, to Balaam through the mouth of an ass, and to Gideon by means of a fleece!

However, we cannot wait for such demonstrations before we know we are called by God, for He rarely speaks in an audible way. A call is sensed by conviction, by an impelling, divine urgency from which there is no escape. Paul had just that conviction in Acts 16:10 when, after being hindered in his travels, the answer came and "immediately we sought to go into Macedonia, concluding that God had called us . . ." (NAS). Doors were shut everywhere else. Yes, however you may try to reason against it, you cannot silence the inner voice of the Holy Spirit.

There are some simple tests which will help in such a momentous decision:

1. What evidence is there of fruit in your witness and from your testimony? In what ways can you see the hand of God on your life in blessing? Is there true love for God and a burden to see men and women redeemed by the blood of the Lord Jesus? In other words, are you hungry for fruitfulness in the work of the Kingdom? David Brainerd, working among unresponsive Indians, cried in anguish to the Lord in prayer, "Give me souls, or I die."

2. Are you convinced that your message is adequate? If you have any doubt about that, then you are defeated before you begin. Read Acts 13 and see how the Word of God burned in the hearts of the disciples and through them to those who heard and came to faith in Christ.

3. What is your attitude toward sin? Is it total warfare, or are there areas of compromise in your life? Your attitude toward sin will govern 157 your attitude toward repentance, regeneration, and redemption. A shallow view of sin will mean a shallow view of salvation.

4. What is your attitude toward people? You will spend your life with all kinds of people, those you like and those you may really dislike. Your reaction to them will largely decide your success or failure as a servant of Jesus Christ. If you are easily hurt or resentful, beware, and seek the face of God that you might have the mind of Christ. Scotland has a very interesting national emblem—a thistle surrounded by a motto in Latin: *Nemo me impune lacessit,*—"nobody touches me with impunity." Get a Scotsman's hackles up and you have trouble on your hand! But we are all easily hurt when our egos have been punctured.

5. What is your attitude to fellow workers? Can you be trusted with leadership? Read Mark 10:45 thoughtfully: "For the Son of man did not come to be served but to serve, and to give his life a ransom for many." If you imagine you are the boss or the brains, your little throne will begin to totter, and others will lose respect for you. And what about your attitude to those who oppose you? The words of Jesus are salutary: "Woe to you, when all men speak well of you" (Luke 6:26). The first human instinct is to crush opposition, but that is not the Lord's way. It is far better to win opponents by love and to work with them rather than against them, for a little special attention and love work wonders. "Bless those who curse you, pray for those who mistreat you" (Luke 6:28 NAS).

6. What is your attitude to people of other races and religions? "From now on, therefore, we regard no one from a human point of view," writes Paul in 2 Corinthians 5:16. People from every tribe and nation were born for eternity, and our responsibility is to forget our culture and win them by love, in the spirit of Christ.

7. What is your attitude toward rich people? Would you lower your standards to secure their favor? Fine houses, rich clothing, and big bank accounts do not soften God's demands for repentance. We should neither discriminate against them, nor cheapen the gospel to win their favor.

Consider these tests and weigh up the evidences of the call until you are convinced that it is the Lord Himself who calls you into His royal service.

He Must Be a Choice Man

In Matthew 22:14 Jesus says, "For many are called, but few are chosen," and that last word has the meaning of "choice," separate or pre-

THE MAKING OF A MAN OF GOD

pared. The Shunammite woman in 2 Kings 4:9, commenting on Elisha, said to her husband, "I perceive that this is a holy man of God, who is continually passing our way." A choice man is a holy man, and like a new house he is open for inspection all the time. The servant of the Lord has no inherent immunity from evil; it is necessary to experience temptation and to fight daily to overcome it in order to grow in grace. There must not be a yawning gap between precept and practice. "You who teach others, will you not teach yourself? While you preach against stealing, do you steal?" (Rom. 2:21). An outward profession of faith must be supported by an inward practice of holiness. Christian leaders are not expected to be paragons, but they are expected to be consistent. There is no greater advertisement for the gospel than a life which is thoroughly good, for what touches others about Christians is that they are what they are supposed to be. Many unbelievers put up much higher standards for believers than we do for ourselves—a sobering thought.

Therefore, we must be honest with God and deal with the shady corners of our soul, remembering that the greatest factor for evangelism in any ministry is personal holiness. Two of the greatest dangers which face those in the front line of service for the Lord are money and sex. It is essential to live beyond reproach by the grace given to us. Even the way we speak to a waitress in a restaurant can make its mark. If we are chosen by the Lord (see John 15:16), then we are, by the same token, choice servants, and the consistency of our lives will show itself in many ways:

In the choice of a wife, who must be of the same heart and mind. It is a tragedy when a husband and wife are not both called to the work. Tension and resentment are inevitable. For "how can two walk together, unless they have made an appointment [or unless they be agreed]?" (Amos 3:3). Jesus clearly says, "If two of you agree on earth about anything they ask, it will be done for them by my Father in heaven" (Matt. 18:19).

In family worship, sharing the events of the day before they begin and after they have happened. There are to be no secrets, but perfect oneness.

In all absence of gossip. Never use friends or members of the congregation—or even your family—as illustrations! Be discreet with confidences. I once formed a mutual encouragement fellowship at a time of stress in one of my pastorates. The members subscribed to a simple formula applied before speaking of any person or subject that was perhaps controversial.

T—Is it true?
H—Is it helpful?
I —Is it inspiring?
N—Is it necessary?
K—Is it kind?

If what I am about to say does not pass those tests, I will keep my mouth shut! And it worked!

In handling of money and paying debts. Remember "Owe no one anything except to love one another" (Rom. 13:8). The prompt payment of bills is a silent witness to the honesty and integrity that should characterize the child of God.

He Must Be a Chaste Man

The Christian leader faces many dangers and must be strengthened against them. The missiles the enemy hurls most frequently are self-indulgence, laziness, intemperance, and pride. Perhaps you have your own particular weaknesses, but there are safeguards, and we ignore them at our peril. They may involve sterner discipline than we have ever experienced before, but consider Paul's words, "I do not run aimlessly, I do not box as one beating the air; but I pommel my body and subdue it, lest after preaching to others I myself should be disqualified" (1 Cor. 9:26, 27).

First of all then, communion with God must be a priority. How often we must drive ourselves to it, even after rapturous experiences! How often it can be scamped! Perhaps you can recall times when you have seen the neglected prayer lists, the unopened Bible, the notes of some message only half prepared because the unction of the Holy Spirit has deserted you. Yet we must remember that in every arena of battle there must be an altar of worship. That is the testing point of all Christian ministry. Win there, and heaven opens in blessing. Be defeated there, and life is a weary round of toilsome routine, trying to keep up an appearance of that which is departed, and one day—say it softly—the judgment of God comes upon a prayerless life. There is no use in waiting for a sense of urgency to pray; pray when you feel nothing at all! There are no shortcuts to attaining chasteness before God.

In 1 Chronicles 4:23 we read of some very humble people who "dwelt there with the king for his work." That is the secret: with the King for His work. So often we find ourselves submerged under our own responsibilities, sweating and toiling to get things rolling because we are not abiding in the presence of the King and gaining His strength for His work.

Prayer should be the key that opens the day and the lock that closes the night. A night shift is never as good as a day one, and it is glorious to meet our heavenly Father at the freshness of dawn as we pray over the coming hours and all involved in them, and listen to His orders for the day.

Secondly, it is essential to care for the body, for it is the temple of the Holy Spirit (1 Cor. 6:19). Appetite is a good thing, but it must be restrained. Exercise is good and should be taken regularly. Sometimes we must refuse social engagements in order to spend time with the Lord and also to get sufficient sleep before we awaken to keep the dawn watch with Him. Our lives need discipline or they run to seed and weed like a neglected garden.

Paul's great challenge in Romans 12:1–2 needs daily application. Present your body to the Lord, for it is the only vehicle He has to convey His message, love, and help to a needy world. A story is told of Bishop Taylor Smith, who was a man of substantial size. Each day as he awakened he threw off the covers, stretched himself out on his bed, and said, "For today, Lord, this bed is the altar and I am the sacrifice; Your orders, please." What a way to begin the day!

When I was pastor at Moody Church in Chicago, Dr. A. W. Tozer was my good friend and faithful counselor. Not too long after my arrival in Chicago he phoned me and said, "You may be lonely and in need of a friend with whom to pray and share. Should you wish to do so with me, you will find me any morning between 5:00 and 8:00 from April to October on the south shore of Lake Michigan." Well, it was very early, and the place was some twenty-five miles from where I lived, so I did not go very often. But when I did, I found Dr. Tozer lying face down on the sand before an open Bible. For three hours he kept this tryst with God, and I was humbled to be invited to share this precious time with him. I learned that these hours with God were the secret of his deep and dynamic ministry, which penetrated the minds and hearts of his listeners. When he 161 moved from Chicago to Toronto, we realized there had been in our midst one who was truly called, choice, and chaste—a man of God.

NOTES

Made for Ministry

There are two prevailing views of the Christian life today. One is that once you are saved you become a spectator and watch God work. The other is that you become a servant, involved in God's work. If you had to be honest about your relationship with Jesus Christ, would you be considered a spectator or a servant? Paul paints the accurate biblical portrait of every believer:

> For we are His workmanship, created in Christ Jesus for good works, which God prepared beforehand, that we should walk in them (Eph. 2:10).

We are His workmanship, the masterpiece of Almighty God. Scripture says He created you spiritually in Christ Jesus. When we trusted Him as our Savior, we were spiritually born again. For what? Paul's use of the Greek preposition *for,* meaning *for the purpose of,* is the clue. We were created in Christ for the purpose of good works. We are new creations in Christ Jesus, so redeemed and fashioned that we might live a life which is the unfolding of God's will.

Before we were ever born, God had already determined some tasks for us to accomplish. God has wisely chosen for us to invest our lives in an ongoing scheme of fruitful labor. In essence, Paul declares the believer as uniquely made for ministry, divinely regenerated—not for some mystical, spiritual experience but for heaven-initiated and earthly-activated good deeds.

There are eight distinct principles connected with the biblical view of good works which I will define as personal involvement in the lives of others.

Personal Involvement in the Lives of Others Is the Clear Teaching of the Word of God

> And He gave some as apostles, and some as prophets, and some as evangelists, and some as pastors and teachers, for the equipping of the saints for

the work of service, to the building up of the body of Christ, until we all attain to the unity of the faith, and of the knowledge of the Son of God, to a mature man, to the measure of the stature which belongs to the fulness of Christ (Eph. 4:11–13).

Those gifted in church leadership are endowed so as to equip the saints for ministry and to build up the whole body of Christ. Are you involved today in anybody's life, or any group of people's lives, for the purpose of building them up and encouraging them in their Christian lives? Is your life making a difference in anybody else's life because you see your responsibility to minister to them?

Paul admonishes, "Therefore, my beloved brethren, be steadfast, immovable, always abounding in the work of the Lord, knowing that your [toil] is not in vain in the Lord" (1 Cor. 15:58 NKJV).

What is the work that God has called us to do? He has called us to ministry, to serving. How do we serve God? We serve God by involving ourselves in the lives of other people, "always abounding in the work of the Lord," and· overflowing in ministry to other people.

The New Testament church took excellent care of widows; they even comprised a list of widows. One of the qualifications for being on the church's list was a history of good deeds. It is interesting as he gives the criteria of those who could be recognized as widows:

Let a widow be put on the list only if she is not less than sixty years old, having been the wife of one man, having a reputation for good works; and if she has brought up children, if she has shown hospitality to strangers, if she has washed the saints' feet, if she has assisted those in distress, and if she has devoted herself to every good work (1 Tim. 5:9, 10).

So in order for a widow to be provided for by the New Testament church, she had to have been involved in ministering to other people.

The wealthy likewise had a spiritual mandate for good works.

Instruct those who are rich in this present world not to be conceited or to fix their hope on the uncertainty of riches, but on God who richly supplies us with all things to enjoy. Instruct them to do good, to be rich in good works, to be generous, and ready to share (1 Tim. 6:17, 18).

Everyone, rich or poor, young or old, well known or unknown, is to be involved in ministry. Education, social status, and personality are not the essential ingredients. You do not even have to finish grammar school to encourage and build up others in the faith. Every believer is equipped in some manner by the Spirit to serve others.

God can create everything that He or His church will ever need. But He has chosen to carry on His work through the labor of His people.

Personal Involvement in the Lord's Work Is Essential if We Are Going to Follow Christ

A Christian does not just believe in Jesus Christ in order to receive salvation but patterns his life after the Lord Jesus Christ.

What kind of life did Jesus live? What did He do? Jesus Christ was a teacher. He shared with the woman at the well and led her to receive Him as the living water. Jesus Christ was a comforter. Jesus Christ was a rescuer. He involved Himself in people's lives when they were in trouble. When the apostles were out on the sea in the storm, He came walking on the water to rescue them from almost certain death in that storm. Everywhere you see Jesus Christ in the Bible, He is always reaching out to people.

The only time He is not helping others is when He is talking to the Father. Even then, He is drawing strength to go out again and pour Himself into somebody's life. Luke summarized Jesus' earthly ministry in this succinct, dynamic statement:

> You know of Jesus of Nazareth, how God anointed Him with the Holy Spirit and with power, and how He went about doing good, and healing all who were oppressed by the devil; for God was with Him (Acts 10:38).

The average believer feels this way: "Well, you know, I've got a job. I work five or six days a week, eight or ten or twelve hours a day, and I don't have much time for God." Wait a minute! The day you trusted Jesus Christ as your personal Savior, from God's point of view, your priority became ministry. Your vocation became a means to provide food, clothing, shelter, and other things that you need or desire in order to carry on your ministry successfully.

Now the average businessman or woman in this country does not even begin to think that way. Their job is their life. The truth is that Jesus Christ is your life. Your purpose for being here is to glorify God, and one of the means we glorify Him is through good works to others. "Let your light shine before men in such a way that they may see your good works, and glorify your Father who is in heaven" (Matt. 5:16).

Jesus did not come to be ministered to, but to minister. His public ministry involved people from every walk of life—harlots, publicans, tax collectors, fishermen. Now if He came to serve and if we are His followers, we will be involved in the lives of other people.

Think about this: If God created you in Christ Jesus for the purpose of becoming personally involved in the lives of other people, your purpose is to live here and glorify God. You might as well go ahead and die and go to heaven if you opt out of Spirit-directed ministry. For what other purpose is God leaving you on earth? For now that your sins have been forgiven, and your name written in the Lamb's book of life, your destiny is heaven.

Personal Involvement in the Lives of Others Means Utilizing our Spiritual Gifts to Serve Others

Gifts are given by God to glorify Him and serve others. There are several cornerstone passages addressing the issue of spiritual gifts.

And He gave some as apostles, and some as prophets, and some as evangelists, and some as pastors and teachers, for the equipping of the saints for the work of service, to the building up of the body of Christ; until we all attain to the unity of the faith, and of the knowledge of the Son of God, to a mature man, to the measure of the stature which belongs to the fulness of Christ (Eph. 4:11–13).

And since we have gifts that differ according to the grace given to us, let each exercise them accordingly: if prophecy, according to the proportion of his faith; if service, in his serving; or he who teaches, in his teaching; or he who exhorts, in his exhortation; he who gives, with liberality; he who leads, with diligence; he who shows mercy, with cheerfulness (Rom. 12:6–8).

Now concerning spiritual gifts, brethren, I do not want you to be unaware. You know that when you were pagans, you were led astray to the dumb idols, however you were led. Therefore I make known to you, that no one speaking by the Spirit of God says, "Jesus is accursed"; and no one can say, "Jesus is Lord," except by the Holy Spirit. Now there are varieties of gifts, but the same Spirit. And there are varieties of ministries, and the same

Lord. And there are varieties of effects, but the same God who works all things in all persons. But to each one is given the manifestation of the Spirit for the common good (1 Cor. 12:1–7).

Here is the common denominator: God does not give spiritual gifts to exalt us or to make us feel better. He gives spiritual gifts for the common good, that we may exercise our gifts in ministry to others and in order to fulfill His will for our lives. God is glorified by what He does through us in the lives of others.

God's spiritual gifts do not require a certain amount of education. One of the most effective witnesses I ever met never finished the sixth grade. The cultivation of your gift is the issue. If you do not know what your gift is, it is your responsibility to seek God and the counsel of wise, mature Christian leaders and discover it.

God has given you a special gift and has provided a way for you to exercise that gift. What are you doing with it? The very gift itself is an act of God's grace. The equipping, cultivation, and the use of that gift is all by God's grace. And God has given gifts to meet every need of His church and His people, whether it be giving, teaching, singing, or working in the nursery. There are no unimportant places of service in the kingdom of God.

One of these days you are going to stand before Almighty God. In 2 Corinthians 5:10, Paul warns that we are going to give an account of the way we have used the gifts and talents God has given us by His grace and how we spent our time on earth. If we have been faithful He will reward us for the way we fulfilled that ministry.

Peter condenses the whole story of spiritual gifts: As each one has received a special gift, employ it in serving one another, as good stewards of the manifold grace of God (1 Peter 4:10). All that God requires of us is faithfulness in discharging our ministry.

Personal Involvement in the Lives of Others Is the Same as Serving Jesus

Then the King will say to those on His right, "Come, you who are blessed of My Father, inherit the kingdom prepared for you from the foundation of the world: For I was hungry, and you gave Me something to eat; I was thirsty, and you gave Me drink; I was a stranger, and you invited Me in;

naked, and you clothed Me; I was sick, and you visited Me; I was in prison, and you came to Me." Then the righteous will answer Him, saying, "Lord, when did we see You hungry, and feed You, or thirsty, and give You drink? And when did we see You a stranger, and invite You in, or naked, and clothe You? And when did we see You sick, or in prison, and come to You?" And the King will answer and say to them, "Truly I say to you, to the extent that you did it to one of these brothers of Mine, even the least of them, you did it to Me" (Matt. 25: 34–40).

When we help clothe someone else, it is like clothing Christ. When we give someone a cold drink, He says it is the same as doing it to Him. Whenever we become involved in ministering to other people, whatever form it may take, we are ministering to Jesus.

The third chapter of Colossians covers the relationship of husbands and wives, children and parents, and slaves and masters. In each instance, responsibility is rendered "as unto the Lord" (v. 23). When we serve each other we are serving the Lord. When a husband is loving his wife, he is loving the Lord. When children are obeying their parents, they are obeying the Lord Jesus Christ. When an employee does a good job, it is as if he were doing it for the Lord. When an employer treats his employees properly and serves them, it is as if he were doing it unto the Lord. All of our service is to be done enthusiastically, excitedly, as we are doing it to Almighty God Himself. The only way we can serve the Lord is to get involved in somebody else's life, and when we do, He says we do that work as unto Him. As believers we should walk into our jobs on Monday morning—whether it is raining, snowing, sleeting, hailing, or foggy—and work heartily unto the Lord.

Personal Involvement in the Lives of Others Is Necessary in Order to Experience the Power of the Holy Spirit

By the power of the Holy Spirit I mean that divine enablement which equips us to do what otherwise we could not do.

Why should God empower us with the Holy Spirit?

In order that we might be involved in the lives of other people! In every verse and passage in the New Testament that mentions the power of the Holy Spirit, we find that power is given for ministering, serving, and working for the Lord. The Holy Spirit does not empower us for some experience. Rather, the Holy Spirit fills us and shapes us into the likeness of Christ, anointing us and flowing through us.

As a thirteen-year-old child, I was greatly influenced by my Sunday school teacher. When I delivered newspapers up and down a certain street, He would stop every once in a while, pull his car over to the curb, and talk with me. He would always buy a paper from me, even though he got one at his home. He was involving himself in my life, encouraging me, loving me, taking the time, even if it was only five minutes to say hello and to thank me for coming to Sunday school.

You can bake a cake in the power of the Holy Spirit when it is motivated to bear witness for Jesus Christ and God will use it to get the gospel to people. Just giving people things is not sufficient. You give it to them in the name of Jesus Christ, in the power of the Holy Spirit. God can take a simple piece of clothing, given in the name of Jesus Christ, and transform a person's life.

Why does the Holy Spirit come with power? The Holy Spirit comes with power in order to equip us for ministry. We may ask God to anoint us, but we have no reason to ask unless we have a work to do. As long as we think we can do it in our own strength, we will never be filled with the Spirit. The power of the Holy Spirit comes to unctionize and equip us for the ministry to which God has called us. It is a supernatural work to be done under the supernatural power of God.

Personal Involvement in the Lives of Others Brings Joy and Fulfillment and Thereby Growth toward Maturity

To be emotionally healthy, all of us need a sense of worth, and confidence. When we become involved with other people, a sense of belonging develops. As God begins to use us in the lives of others, our sense of worthiness increases. We are valuable to God, as the Holy Spirit helps us succeed in what we are doing.

First John, chapter one, contains a jewel of truth regarding personal ministry to others: "What we have seen and heard we proclaim to you also, that you also may have fellowship with us; and indeed our fellowship is with the Father, and with His Son Jesus Christ. And these things we write, so that our joy may be made complete" (vv. 3–4).

The apostle John was excited about the life of service. There is no reason for a Christian ever to be bored. How can you be bored when your name is written in the Lamb's Book of Life, when you are filled with the Holy Spirit, when there is a lost world to win, when you have been commissioned by Jesus Christ? How can you be bored when the power of the Holy Spirit is available to you? How can you be bored when there are people hurting, needing somebody to help them? How can you be bored, unless you are spiritually deaf, blind, or lack compassion?

Third John, verses three and four, further describes the thrill of selfless ministry: "For I was very glad when brethren came and bore witness to your truth, that is, how you are walking in truth. I have no greater joy than this, to hear of my children walking in the truth."

John felt great joy when he learned that his converts were walking in the truth. A great sense of fulfillment, joy, contentment and inspiration is activated when you get involved in somebody else's life, whether it is in your office, in your home, or to a stranger.

Personal Involvement in the Lives of Others
May Take the Form of Intercessory Prayer and Witnessing

Every morning as you go before Almighty God in prayer, He can use you to alter the kingdoms of the world, to snatch somebody from the kingdom of darkness and set them in the kingdom of light. Or God can use you as a soul-winner to explain the plan of salvation.

There is no telling what God can do through your life if you will allow Him to do it, if you are willing.

God is not asking you to work for Him in your own strength, your own wisdom, or out of your own experience. He is asking you to do it out of a power that He provides if you will but trust Him. God assumes the responsibility of equipping and empowering you. That renders us inexcusable.

Personal Involvement in the Lives of Others
Is the Normal Response of Genuine Faith

What use is it, my brethren, if a man says he has faith, but he has no works? Can that faith save him? If a brother or sister is without clothing and in need of daily food, and one of you says to them, "Go in peace, be warmed and be filled," and yet you do not give them what is necessary for their body, what use is that? Even so faith, if it has no works, is dead, being by itself.

But someone will say, "You have faith, and I have works; show me your faith without the works, and I will show you my faith by my works" (James 2:14–18).

Paul's great emphasis is justification by faith. It is faith, not faith plus works, that saves us. James, on the other hand, takes a different viewpoint. He says yes, you are saved by faith, but the quality and nature of the faith that saves you will be evidenced by work. So he is talking about genuine faith that gives proof of its validity. If somebody tried you in a court of law for being a Christian, would there be enough evidence to convict you? Could your coworkers testify that you are a true follower of Jesus? In your school or university, do your fellow students know you as a Christian because of your words and actions? Nobody is excused from being personally involved in some form of ministry.

In what way, how, when, are you involved in some form of ministry in anybody's life? Do you know what the Bible talks about when believers stand before the judgment seat of Christ? Personal involvement in the lives of other people, that's what it is all going to be about. I wonder how many blank pages will be turned in your life, or will God open the book on your life and it will look just like this Bible? Hallelujah! Praise the Lord! Glory to God!

If you love the living God who saved you, and you accept the truth of Scripture, do you not agree that you need to make a personal commitment today? You may want to say it in this fashion: "Lord, today I commit myself to become involved in personal ministry anywhere, anytime, anyway as You guide and empower me. I choose to be available from this moment on." Your Christian life will be transformed.

NOTE

Scripture quotations in this article are from the NEW AMERICAN STANDARD VERSION of the Bible. Copyright © 1960, 1962, 1963, 1968, 1971, 1972, 1973, 1975, 1977 by the Lockman Foundation.

A Strength in Difficulty

One of the most notable trials in history was the "Monkey Trial" of John T. Scopes in 1925. Later a stage play was written about the trial entitled *Inherit The Wind.*[1] Two major characters in the actual trial and in the stage play were a Chicago lawyer named Clarence Darrow and the United States politician William Jennings Bryan. In the play Darrow says: "Progress has never been a bargain. You've got to pay for it. Sometimes I think there is a man behind the counter who says, 'All right you can have a telephone, but you will have to give up your privacy for the charm of distance. Madam, yes you may vote, but at a price. You lose the right to retreat beyond a powder puff or a petticoat. Mister, you may conquer the air, but the birds will lose their wonder, and the clouds will smell like gasoline.' Darwin moved us forward to a hilltop where we could look back and see the way from which we came. But for this view, this insight, this knowledge, we must abandon our faith and pleasant poetry of Genesis."

William Jennings Bryan replied, "We must not abandon faith, because faith is the most important thing in the world."

The same debate rages on today. In the August 3 issue of the *Washington Post Weekly,* an interesting feature article focused on the John Webster family from Mobile, Alabama. A year earlier John and Sue and their children, David and Laura, were responsible for a similar trial in Alabama which banned forty-four textbooks from the Alabama curriculum. A higher court later overturned the decision, and it was appealed to the Supreme Court. The Websters have received a great deal of criticism and, as usual, those who believe in creationism are characterized as red-necks, bare-footed, ignorant, Bible-believing, tobacco-chewing dummies. When the *Washington Post Weekly* came down to interview the Websters, they came away with an article that sounded more like one in *Moody Monthly.* I was amazed when I read the article because it admitted that the Websters are on to something. They are struggling with the same dilemmas facing all America. Although they are ridiculed, the Websters have the answer so many Americans are seeking. They know who they are and they know the whys of their lives because they all had had a born-again experience with Jesus Christ. Thus, they had a foundation in their life to stand on to deal with the issues that plague every one of us. Sue asked, "Why is it that there are so many teenage suicides, pregnancies, drugs, and alcohol problems, and the world's way is doing nothing about it, and all they do is criticize us for being simplistic?" But the world's way is not working. The state brought in a special witness, Robert Cole, who is from Harvard University and is one of the most eminent child psychiatrists in the country. He studied the textbooks, got on the witness stand, and said, "The stuff is junk. I wouldn't want my kids to read it and you ought not to have your kids read it, either." So much for the expert witness.

We are going to look now at Shadrach, Meshach, and Abed-Nego—Daniel's three friends who were able to escape from a fiery furnace because they had the courage to stand up for what they believed in a world that did not believe it.

Daniel and his friends had been brought from Israel to captivity in Babylon. King Nebuchadnezzar decided to erect an image of himself and required everyone in the country to worship it. It was a curious looking image. As you translate out those cubits and all those strange sounding dimensions, it was nine feet wide and ninety feet tall.

Nebuchadnezzar required everyone in the land to bow down and to worship this image of himself and let it become his god. Daniel's three friends refused to bow down and worship Nebuchadnezzar's image. They just would not do it. Some of the Chaldeans, already jealous of these Hebrews who were doing so well in their land, exposed them. So let us first consider the trial of their faith.

The Trial of Their Faith

Shadrach, Meshach, and Abed-Nego lived in a world that *defied God's principles*. The people of their world had seen God reveal the dreams of Nebuchadnezzar. They had seen principles of Scripture set forth in their land. And yet these people defiantly set up an image contrary to the things of God and defied God's principles. Our world is not too different from that today. One of the textbooks in question in the Mobile trial says that morality is not some word given from a supreme being or from a religious context. Rather, morality is what the majority of the people think it is at

173

any given time. Of course, the majority of people could vote to murder or steal or anything else and, left to themselves, they probably would. Likewise Shadrach, Meshach, and Abed-Nego lived in an atmosphere where the very principles of God were defied.

Shadrach, Meshach, and Abed-Nego lived in a world which *denied God's power.* The people around them had already seen God help their king, Nebuchadnezzar, yet they set up a graven image instead of worshiping God. They said, "We are going to worship this unknown source, and we are not going to let God's power even be recognized in our land." We live in a world today that ignores the power of God. Too often this attitude spills over into the church, and the church ignores the power of God. A few years ago I visited a man in the hospital. He was having open-heart surgery, and his family asked me to go see him beforehand. He had not sent for me, but I went to see him as his family requested. "I would like to pray for you before you go into surgery" I said. He replied, "Well, if it would make you feel better, go right on." I responded, "I don't feel bad to start with. It's you who are sick." He said, "I don't need prayer."

Shadrach, Meshach, and Abed-Nego were living in a world that *despised God's people.* We don't like to think about that. But it is very evident that certain Chaldeans hated these men for believing in God. And today, despite some of the popularity the evangelical churches have enjoyed in the last twenty years, God's people are hated by the sponsors and producers of the world system. If you are really in love with the Lord, the world hates you.

Recently I heard a most interesting story about a newspaper's investigation into the finances of a large Christian organization. The newspaper ran an article that accused the organization of dishonesty with its money. The organization denied the accusation that had been previously printed in the paper and was able to provide evidence that no wrongdoing had occurred. When the Christian organization called for a retraction of the accusation, the newspaper's response was not only negative but hostile.

One person from the paper essentially said that he resented Christians and that there would be no retraction. He was willing to allow the false charges to stand since so many would believe them to be true.

It happens. Jesus said, "If the world hates you, you know that it hated Me before it hated you. If you were of the world, the world would love its own. Yet because you are not of the world, but I chose you out of the world, therefore the world hates you" (John 15:18–19). Whether we recognize it on a daily basis or not, our faith is on trial, just as surely as that of Shadrach, Meshach, and Abed-Nego.

The Testimony of Their Faith

Nebuchadnezzar was furious. Even after they were given a second chance, Shadrach, Meshach and Abed-Nego refused to bow down and worship his image. He threatened, "When all these instruments start playing, I want you to bow down and worship my image, then everything will be all right. But if not, I am going to throw you in the fiery furnace."

Notice their reply: "Shadrach, Meshach, and Abed-Nego answered . . . the king, 'O, Nebuchadnezzar, we have no need to answer you in this matter'" (Dan. 3:16). This is *consistency* of faith! Jesus said in Luke 9:62, "No one, having put his hand to the plow, and looking back, is fit for the kingdom of God." Martin Luther, the great father of the Reformation, stood at the Diet of Worms and was asked over and over again to recant! But he insisted, "Here I stand, so help me God, I can do no other."[1]

Secondly, we see the *confidence* of their faith: "If that is the case, our God whom we serve is able to deliver us from the burning fiery furnace, and He will deliver us from your hand, O king" (Dan. 3:17). Do you have that confident faith? Regardless of the pressures and trials and circumstances in your life, do you have the confidence that God will deliver you? Shadrach, Meshach, and Abed-Nego said, "You know you may throw us in the fiery furnace, but frankly we don't care, because our God is able to deliver us."

Some of you know what I am talking about. You have been in the fiery furnace or you may be in the fiery furnace right now.

But we also see the *contentment* of their faith. "But if not, [if God chooses not to deliver us] let it be known to you, O king, that we do not serve your gods, nor will we worship the gold image which you have set up" (Dan. 3:18). Their relationship to God was not based on what God did for them. They were content to be with God whether they were in the furnace or out of the furnace. What about your faith? Is it consistent, confident, and content?

The Triumph of Their Faith

Shadrach, Meshach, and Abed-Nego were delivered *to* the flames. We might like the story better if God had another way. But there are three very important words that go with this text. They were delivered to the flames. They went to the place of suffering. Sometimes, regardless of our prayer, faith, trust, or commitment, God's plan is for us to be delivered to the flames.

Peter says:

> Beloved, do not think it strange concerning the fiery trial which is to try you, as though some strange thing happened to you; but rejoice to the extent that you partake of Christ's sufferings, that when His glory is revealed, you may also be glad with exceeding joy. If you are reproached for the name of Christ, blessed are you, for the Spirit of glory and of God rests upon you. On their part He is blasphemed, but on your part He is glorified. But let none of you suffer as a murderer, a thief, an evildoer, or as a busybody in other people's matters. Yet if anyone suffers as a Christian, let him not be ashamed, but let him glorify God in this matter. For the time has come for judgment to begin at the house of God; and if it begins with us first, what will be the end of those who do not obey the gospel of God? "If the righteous one is scarcely saved, where will the ungodly and the sinner appear?" Therefore, let those who suffer according to the will of God commit their souls to Him in doing good, as to a faithful Creator (1 Peter 4:12–19).

My dear friends, there are times in our lives when the very triumph of our faith is to be delivered to the flames. The rest of the story is not pretty. They bound them, tied them, and got the furnace so hot that the men who threw them in fell and died. Sometimes it is God's will for us to be delivered to the furnace.

I want you to also notice they were delivered *in* the flames. Nebuchadnezzar was astonished. He arose in haste, saying to the counselors, "Did we not cast three men bound into the midst of the fire?" And they answered and said to the king, "True O king." "Look!" he answered, "I see four men loose, walking in the midst of the fire; and they are not hurt, and the form of the fourth is like the Son of God" (Dan. 3:24–25). So sometimes it is God's will to deliver us *in* the flames and to be with us. In Hebrews we are reminded of God's promise "never to leave or forsake us" (13:5). It was in a time of storm that the angel of the Lord came and stood beside Paul and said, "Do not be afraid" (Acts 27:24). Sometimes we go all the way into the furnace and, in the furnace, we see the Son of God. If Shadrach, Meshach, and Abed-Nego had avoided the furnace, they never would have seen Jesus face to face in the furnace. God promises He will be with us in the furnace of trouble and will deliver us (see Ps. 91:15).

Shadrach, Meshach, and Abed-Nego were delivered in the flames and they were delivered *from* the flames. When Nebuchadnezzar saw the Son of God walking around in the flames, he was convinced. "How many men did we throw in the furnace? Three, I see four, and the fourth one looks like the Son of God. Turn the gas off. Let them out, let them out." That's a good testimony, too. Psalm 34:17 and 19 says, "The righteous cry out, and the Lord hears, and delivers them out of all their troubles. Many are the afflictions of the righteous. But the Lord delivers him out of them all."

The triumph of our faith could be in any one of these three areas: our delivery *to* the flames, our delivery *in* the flames, or our delivery *from* the flames. To have that kind of strength in difficulty is to have the kind of commitment Shadrach, Meshach, and Abed-Nego had: consistent, confident, and contented faith. Then nothing will shake us. Nothing! Because "if God is for us, who can be against us?" (Rom. 8:31). Yes, "In all these things we are more than conquerors through Him who loved us" (Rom. 8:37).

NOTES

1. Jerome Lawrence and Robert E. Lee, *Inherit the Wind* (New York: Random House, 1955).
   Scripture quotations in this article are from the NEW KING JAMES VERSION of the Bible. Copyright © 1979, 1980, 1982 by Thomas Nelson, Inc., Publishers.

The New Testament and Revival

TED S. RENDALL

D oes the New Testament authorize us to pray and plead for the revival of the church?
        I raise that question because it is sometimes argued that revival
is essentially and exclusively an Old Testament concept. The New
Testament, we are told, does not speak to the matter of the revival and
renewal of God's people collectively.

But is this truly the case?

Bible students agree that the Old Testament contains pictures, patterns,
and principles of spiritual revival; indeed, promises and prayers relating
to revival are scattered throughout its pages in a wide variety of literary
forms, including history, poetry and prophecy.[1]

But at first glance the New Testament seems strangely lacking in such
materials. It is as if revival is not to be asked for at the throne of grace in
this dispensation.[2]

Some years ago, after having preached a message on revival, I received
the following interesting letter from a listener:

> "Revive" and "reviving" are Old Testament words. However, the quicken-
> ing of the saints is a characteristic of the normal New Testament assembly. It
> is a continuous state. This is due largely to the stress laid upon the weekly
> remembrance of the Lord, the place given to pure quiet worship, the atten-
> tion given to public reading, to exhortation, teaching and following the as-
> sembly pattern in Acts and Paul's epistles . . . This constant state of revival
> is seen among any company of saints who are willing to pay the price of
> obedience to God's Word.[3]

But not all the fellowships that practice these forms of worship are
really in a condition of revival. The fact, documented by the history of
revival, is that spiritual renewal does not depend on one form of worship
or fellowship. "God shows no partiality" (Acts 10:34) when men and
women are crying out for reality.

The question, therefore, is: Does the New Testament teach us to expect periods of revival in the life and ministry of the church in this dispensation? In other words, is revival characteristic of God's dealings with us as it was with His people in the days of the Old Covenant?

The Theme of Revival in the New Testament

We must first deal with the theme of revival as it is developed historically in the New Testament. If we do not grasp the full scope and sweep of the New Testament, we may conclude that it has nothing to say about revival.

Generally among conservative scholars, the time span covered by the books of the New Testament is estimated to be about one hundred years. This covers approximately the period from the announcement of Christ's birth to the Apocalypse of the apostle John. Of that century we can refer to the church as having been in existence for about sixty-five years. During these years the Gospels, Acts, the apostolic letters, and the Book of Revelation were composed and circulated.

We would not expect that in the Gospels there would be any direct teaching about the revival of the church for the simple reason that the church had not yet been established in its pentecostal form. Any reference to revival would have to be prediction.

In the Acts of the Apostles the church of Christ is established and expanding. While it would not be correct to say that the church during this period was without problems, the spiritual condition of the churches was generally healthy. Acts 9:31 gives this description: "Then the churches throughout all Judea, Galilee, and Samaria had peace and were edified. And walking in the fear of the Lord and in the comfort of the Holy Spirit, they were multiplied." That surely is a description of the church as God intended it.

In the letters of the New Testament (Romans to Jude) we find instructions relating to particular problems facing the churches scattered as they were throughout the Roman Empire. In many of these letters there are solemn warnings about spiritual decline and false doctrine, but normally the churches are seen as vibrant and victorious. The church in Thessalonica, for example, is held up by the apostle Paul as a model church for its worship, work, and witness (see 1 Thess. 1:2–7). When we come to the Book of Revelation, which some commentators claim was written by the apostle John as late as the last decade of the first century, we find

179

that the churches are experiencing lovelessness and lukewarmness—all conditions needing repentance and renewal.

A careful reading of Christ's messages to the seven churches of Asia Minor (see Rev. 1–3) will reveal that all was not well internally in those fellowships of God's people. From this standpoint the seven letters, dictated by the risen Lord of the churches, may be considered as revival letters.[4]

The church at Ephesus, for example, was told that the ascended Lord was grieved by her spiritual condition: "Nevertheless I have this against you, that you have left your first love" (Rev. 2:4). Whether this "first love" is to be interpreted as love for God or love for fellow Christians may be debated. What is clear is that Christ, the Lord of the churches, was deeply offended by the spiritual decline.

Thus repeatedly the risen Lord calls upon the churches to repent (see Rev. 2:5, 16, 21, 22; 3:3, 19). Since repentance is the prelude to revival,[5] we conclude that Christ is calling upon these churches to take the first step toward spiritual renewal and restoration.

It is important to note that these appeals of the risen Lord are not primarily to individuals but to the churches considered as groups of believers. In the case of the church at Laodicea, which is described as being in a pitiful spiritual condition, Christ does offer to fellowship with individuals who are prepared to receive Him in the midst of apostasy, but normally His appeals are to believers as a whole.

We can now outline the elements of the theme of revival as developed in the New Testament:

1. It was not until the closing years of the first century that the need of revival became apparent and urgent.

2. In the last years of the apostle John, the risen Lord of the church called upon His people to repent—the first step in genuine revival.

3. This appeal was addressed to the churches collectively, although there was a message for individual believers as well.

The Theology of Revival in the New Testament

Is there, then, an identifiable theology of revival in the New Testament Scriptures? We believe there is, and that this theology may be set forth in a series of key concepts. Rather than deriving its basic ideas narrowly from Revelation 1–3, the substance of this theology calls upon the leading themes of the New Testament as a whole. In this way revival is seen not as an optional but as an organic part of the life of the Christian and of the church.

The New Testament announces that those who are the people of God have been delivered "from the dominion of darkness and brought us into the kingdom of the Son" (Col. 1:13 NIV). Christ the Passover Lamb has been sacrificed, thus providing the judicial basis for God's redemption of those who believe in Jesus as the sin-bearing Lamb of God (see 1 Cor. 5:7; John 1:29; and 1 Peter 1:18–19). Christ gave Himself "to rescue us from the present evil age" (Gal. 1:4 NIV), and to make us a "chosen people, a royal priesthood, a holy nation, a people belonging to God" (1 Pet. 2:9 NIV). In his initial doxology the apostle John described those loved by God and loosed from the shackles of their sin by Christ's blood as "a kingdom and priests to serve his God and Father" (Rev. 1:6 NIV).

Redeemed by God from the bondage of sin (see 1 Cor. 6:19, 20), the church is called upon to demonstrate in worship, witness, and works the fact that it is God's agent in the world, the body of Christ, the ascended and glorified Lord (see Matt. 5:13–16; 1 Peter 2:9, 10; Titus 3:8, 14). By faithfully undertaking their Christian duties "without complaining," the people of God will manifest themselves as "blameless and pure, children of God without fault in a crooked and depraved generation, in which [they] shine like stars in the universe as [they] hold out the word of life" (Phil. 2:14–16). This is the ethical and social dimension of the Christian life which God's people must demonstrate before a watching world.

But Christians are not called upon to live and serve in their own power. Before His ascension to God's right hand (see 1 Peter 3:22), the Lord Jesus promised His disciples that they would receive divine dynamic after the Holy Spirit came to them on the day of Pentecost (see Acts 1:8 and Acts 2:1–4). It is for this reason that the church is considered to be the community of the Spirit (see 1 Cor. 12:12, 13). Each believer, at the moment of regeneration (see Titus 3:5, 6), receives the gift of the Spirit of the glorified Jesus (see Rom. 8:9)—the distinctive pentecostal gift. This indwelling of the believer by the Spirit enables us to say with the apostle Paul: "I have been crucified with Christ and I no longer live, but Christ lives in me" (Gal. 2:20). Christ is now the believer's life (see Col. 3:4).

However, glorious as this message of spiritual rebirth and reception of the Spirit of Jesus is, the New Testament teaches that Christians, individually and collectively, may suffer a decline in their experience of the Spirit's fullness or in their expression of the Spirit's fruit. The possession of the Spirit does not by itself automatically guarantee the plenitude of the Spirit. Believers thus need to be exhorted again and again to "be filled with the Spirit" (Eph. 5:18). This means that the reception of the Spirit must be accompanied by the reign of the Spirit in the lives of believers (see Rom. 8:9–16 and Gal. 5:16, 18, and 25). This tragic decline may be due to the power of internal factors—personal disobedience to the known will of God, indulgence in the desires of the flesh—or to the pressure of external forces such as false teaching and the persecution of a hostile government.

When Christians are in spiritual decline, when they have grieved God's indwelling Spirit (see Eph. 4:30), when they are not walking in the light (see 1 John 1:7), when they have been contaminated by sin (see 2 Cor. 7:1), they need to be revived in their walk with God. Thus Christ comes to the church in decline and through His Word makes demands of His people. That Word is like a sword, sharp and piercing (see Rev. 1:16, Eph. 6:17). To the church at Ephesus, for example, Christ says: "Remember the height from which you have fallen! Repent and do the things you did at first. If you do not repent, I will come to you and remove your lampstand from its place" (Rev. 2:5). Remember, repent, repeat—these imperatives form the demand of Christ, and this demand is made more urgent by the possibility of judgment. Christ warns that He will act judicially to register His disapproval of the church in decline by removing its lampstand.

When confronted by Christ's searching demands, God's people must make a decision. They must take Christ's warning seriously and change their attitude toward those things which caused the decline in their love for God and in their fellowship with Him. This act of repentance will demonstrate the sincerity of their desire to be renewed in faith, love, holiness, and victory.

This decision, while it may be undertaken collectively, is also intensely individual. This is clearly brought out in a vivid word picture in Revelation. We recognize that there is a legitimate application of this statement in the preaching of the gospel, yet the verse primarily refers to Christ's offer of renewed fellowship to any responsive believer within a lukewarm body of believers.[6] Christ states: "Those whom I love I rebuke and discipline. So be earnest and repent. Here I am! I stand at the door and knock. If anyone hears my voice and opens the door, I will come in and eat with him, and he with me" (Rev. 3:19–20). Here the revival of a relationship that has cooled is illustrated in terms of two people eating together around a common table.

We come full cycle when we observe that the purpose of revival is the ongoing realization of the initial reason for God's work in the lives of His people. Through revival God's backslidden people are restored to a right relationship with God and are delivered from the shameful condition brought about by their failure (see Rev. 3:17, 18). Revival, therefore, includes the renewal of all that was lost through compromise with sin. Revival holds the promise of renewed fellowship, freedom, and fruitfulness (see 1 John 1:7–9).

When we use the word *cycle,* students of the revivals of the Old Testament will recall the pattern established so frequently in the history of Israel. The book of Judges, for example, records a series of spiritual renewals, each manifesting the same pattern. This cycle includes the following elements: God's people enjoy God's favor; they forsake Him and follow idols; they experience God's judgment; they cry out for deliverance; and God graciously delivers them from the hand of their enemies.

The pattern in the New Testament church varies little from this cyclic experience of God's people in the Old Testament. Because each generation must seek God afresh, there is always the possibility of spiritual decline; at the same time there is always the possibility of spiritual revival and renewal.

The Tide of Revival in the New Testament

The symbol of the tide, while not a biblical image,[7] is a most useful one for the conceptualization of the need and nature of revival.[8]

On the day of Pentecost the church experienced God's flood tide. While in reading the Acts account we must always distinguish between the incidental and the fundamental in the experience of the disciples, there can be little doubt that the crowning blessing of Pentecost was the fullness of the Holy Spirit. This indeed is how the apostle Peter interpreted the phenomena of Pentecost: "God has raised this Jesus to life, and we are all witnesses of the fact. Exalted to the right hand of God, he has received from the Father the promised Holy Spirit, and has poured out what you now see and hear" (Acts 2:32).

This high tide of divine life was maintained in the experience of the 183 early disciples by constant refillings. We read in Acts 2:4 that all of the disciples present in the room "were filled with the Holy Spirit." But in Acts 4:31 they are again "all filled with the Holy Spirit." God's desire for His people is that they continuously experience and express the fullness of divine life.

As we have seen, however, by the end of the apostolic age, the tide of divine life and blessing was ebbing. A close examination of the seven sample churches in chapters two and three of Revelation, however, will reveal that God's people had not all been reduced to the same level of spiritual decline. Just as the tide recedes at different speeds in different places, so in our churches the tide of divine life withdraws not suddenly and dramatically, but gradually and with a great deal of variation due to the spiritual conditions present in each church.

The seven churches of Asia Minor illustrate this fact. Some churches receive commendation without censure (for example, the church in Philadelphia); others receive commendation and censure (for example, the church in Ephesus); and one receives nothing but censure (the church in Laodicea).

This was the sad situation in the closing decade of the first century. Later church history is the story of God's tide ebbing and flowing. Where hearts have been open to the working of God, the tide has flowed in and brought renewal. All through church history we may trace the impact of God's tide of life and power. In times of declension the tide has receded; in times of awakening the tide has flowed in with impressive results.

Three aspects of the flood tide imagery need to be emphasized to the church today:

1. We need the incoming tide of divine life. While there are encouraging signs, the church worldwide needs revival. The cause of God will only be furthered as the church wakes up and shoulders her responsibility before God (see Rev. 3:2-3). The challenge of an unreached world can only be met by a church filled with the life and power of God.

2. God has promised the incoming tide of divine life. The exaltation of Christ to God's right hand guaranteed the gift of the Spirit to successive generations of believers. The present ministry of our great High Priest is the assurance that we can "be filled with all the fullness of God" (Eph. 3:19).

3. The condition for the incoming tide of divine life is heart repentance. We may affirm that repentance is the missing note of evangelical preaching today. Prayer and preaching, too, play an important part in revival, but the prayer must be characterized by the spirit of repentance, and the preaching must call God's people to their knees in brokenness and contrition.

When the church truly repents and receives the flood tide of God's blessing, we shall experience what the apostle Peter promised his generation in Acts 3:19: "Times of refreshing . . . from the presence of the Lord" (AV).[9] Both the Old and New Testaments announce that God intends to make all things new. Revival, we believe, ushers in times of blessing that point to that ultimate and universal renewal.

NOTES

1. Various authors have written helpfully on the subject of Old Testament revivals. These include: Ernest Baker, *The Revivals of the Bible* (London: Kingsgate, 1906); C. E. Autrey, *Revivals of the Old Testament* (Grand Rapids: Zondervan, 1960); W. M. Smith, *The Glorious Revival Under King Hezekiah* (Grand Rapids: Zondervan, 1936); W. W. Fereday, *Josiah and Revival* (Kilmarnock, Scotland: Ritchies, n.d.); and W. C. Kaiser, Jr., *Quest for Renewal* (Chicago: Moody, 1986).
2. Thus Richard W. DeHaan states: "You cannot find a single promise in the Bible pertaining to revival in the church." This quotation is from his booklet, *How To Have A Revival* (Grand Rapids: Radio Bible Class, 1984), p. 26.
3. Personal letter to the author.
4. Vance Havner was completely in harmony with the spirit of these letters when he wrote *Repent or Else!* (Old Tappan, New Jersey: Revell, 1958), recently reprinted as *Messages on Revival* (Grand Rapids: Baker, n.d.). This series of revival messages is on Revelation 1–3.
5. See J. Edwin Orr, *The Church Must First Repent!* (London: Marshall Morgan & Scott, n.d.), p. 141.
6. Bishop W. W. How (1823–1897) wrote a hymn on this Scripture text, the first verse of which reads:

> O Jesus, Thou are standing
> Outside the fast-closed door,
> In lowly patience waiting
> To pass the threshold o'er:
> Shame on us, Christian brothers,
> His Name and sign who bear,
> O, shame, thrice shame upon us,
> To keep Him standing there.

That interpretation of Revelation 3:20 is more in harmony with the original meaning of the verse than modern evangelistic applications of it.
7. The closest statement of the idea is Isaiah 11:9: "The earth will be full of the knowledge of the Lord as the waters cover the sea." See also Habakkuk 2:14.
8. A. Skevington Wood has developed this symbol in *And With Fire* (London: Pickering &

Inglis, 1958). See chapter 12, "The Tide of Revival." This excellent work on revival was reprinted in 1981 as *Baptized with Fire* (London: Pickering & Inglis).

9. The late J. Edwin Orr wrote: "The best definition of *revival* is the phrase 'Times of refreshing from the presence of the Lord.'" See *The Church Must First Repent!* (London: Marshall Morgan & Scott, n.d.), page 42.

Scripture quotations in this article are from the NEW INTERNATIONAL VERSION of the Bible. Copyright © 1978 by New York International Bible Society

Books by Stephen F. Olford:

Christianity and You
Successful Soul Winning/The Secret of Soul-Winning
*Heart-Cry for Revival/Lord, Open the Heavens!
The Sanctity of Sex
The Living Word
I'll Take the High Road
The Tabernacle: Camping with God
*The Grace of Giving
The Christian Message for Contemporary Man
Going Places with God
Preaching the Word of God

Booklets by Stephen F. Olford:

A Living Faith
Becoming a Child of God
Becoming a Man of God
Becoming a Servant of God
Christian Citizenship
Encounter with Anxiety
Encounter with Fear
Encounter with Loneliness
God's Answer to Vietnam
*Manna in the Morning
Meeting My Master
One Nation Under God
The Basis of Blessing
The Coming New World
The Secret of a Happy Home
The Secret of Strength

*Available in foreign editions
He has also written numerous tracts, poems, hymns, and choruses.

Bibliography on Stephen F. Olford:

de Plata, William. Interview with Stephen F. Olford: Tell It From Calvary. Copyright © 1972 by Calvary Baptist Church, New York City 10019, pp. 115–121.

_____. *Fourteen Years with Dr. Stephen F. Olford at Calvary Baptist Church: 1959–1973.* Published by Calvary Baptist Church, 1973.

Enlow, David. "When the Spirit Became Lord." *My Most Memorable Encounter with God."* Copyright © 1977 by Tyndale House Publishers, Wheaton, Il., pp. 149–57.

Eppinger, Paul D. "Four Great Baptist Preachers and the Theology of Preaching," *Foundations.* Rochester, N.Y.: American Baptist Historical Society 11 (April–June, 1968):117–120.

Joyce, C. A. "Rev. Stephen F. Olford, D.D., Litt.D." *My Call to Preach.* Copyright © Marshall, Morgan & Scott, Ltd., 1968, pp. 69–74.

Kooiman, Helen. "Bessie Santmire Olford, Mother of Stephen F. Olford"; "Heather Brown Olford, Wife of Stephen F. Olford." *Silhouettes: Women Behind Great Men.* Copyright © 1972 by Word, Incorporated, Waco, Texas, pp. 13–29.

Kuhl, Victoria. "A Milestone in the Ministry: A Tribute to 25 Years of Dedicated Service." *Encounter,* Series 1, no. 5 (New York: Calvary Baptist Church, May, 1966), pp. 10–16, 19.

_____. "What Price Popularity?" *Encounter,* vol. 4, no. 3 (Holmes Beach, Fl., July–Sept., 1977), pp. 8–9.

Macaulay, J. C. "Olford: The Media Years: 1959—." *Tell It From Calvary* by William R. de Plata, pp. 97–111.

Olford, Stephen F. *Meeting My Master.* Personal testimony aired on ENCOUNTER-TV.

The Duke Street Story: 1870–1970. Copyright © Harry Young 1970. (London: Lakeland), pp. 73–74, 87–99.

DISTINCTIONS/LECTURESHIPS/MEMBERSHIPS

Special Distinctions:

Channel 11, *WPIX-TV Award* (New York City) in recognition of fifteen dynamic years on television with Encounter, 1960–1975.

Plaques of Appreciation, "Renewal '82"—Manila, Cebu City and Davao City, The Philippines.

Faith and Freedom Award, Religious Heritage of America, 1983.

Who's Who in Religion, 3rd ed., 1985.

Distinguished Service Award, National Religious Broadcasters, for 27 years in radio broadcasting, 1987.

Lectureships:

Swartley Lectures, Eastern Baptist Seminary, Philadelphia, PA.

Christian Life Series (Thomas F. Staley Foundation), Nyack College, Nyack, NY.

Dunlap Lecture Series, Bethany Bible College, Sussex, N.B., Canada.

Short Quarter '74, Columbia Bible College, Columbia, SC.

The Olford Lecture Series, Luther Rice Seminary, Jacksonville, Florida (annual).

Has lectured on preaching at major theological seminaries, Bible colleges, and other schools worldwide.

Memberships:

Fellow of the Royal Geographical Society, London, England.

Life Fellow of The Philosophical Society of Great Britain, Victoria Institute.

Serves on the Council of Reference for numerous Christian organizations.